Holiday Snap

A comedy

Michael Pertwee
and
John Chapman

Samuel French – London
New York – Sydney – Toronto – Hollywood

Please see page iv for further copyright information

HOLIDAY SNAP

First presented at the Yvonne Arnaud Theatre, Guildford with the following cast of characters:

Commander Chittenden (Chitto)	Neil Stacy
Leslie	Keith Barron
Eve	Anita Graham
Henry	John Quayle
Mary	Wanda Ventham
Celia	Eleanor Summerfield
Perky	Royce Mills
Kit	Ginni Barlow

The play was directed by Ray Cooney
Designed by Joe Vanek

The action takes place in the living room of a luxury time-share villa in Portugal

Time—the present

ACT I   Late afternoon in July
ACT II   Immediately following

ACT I

The living-room of a well appointed, brand new villa in Portugal. Marble steps go UL *to big, solid-looking double doors through which (when open) can be seen a porch with bougainvillea and a distant view of mountains.* UR *are french windows opening onto a wide, curved balcony. The tops of pine and palm trees are visible over the parapet of the balcony. Steps* R *on balcony (unseen) lead down to the garden and swimming pool. On wall* DR *an archway leads to a bedroom. Above this archway a door leads to the kitchen. Between french windows and front doors is a trolley with drinks.* US *of trolley is a stool with a food hamper on it. On wall* DL *is a door to another bedroom. Above this bedroom door is a door to a large, walk-in cupboard. The furnishings are cool and modern. The main items of furniture are a large sofa and an armchair. There are at least two occasional tables: on one is a telephone and directory, on another, beside the armchair, is a bowl of fruit and a handbell. There is a wall light and one or two lamps*

As the CURTAIN *rises the stage is empty and in half light. It is late afternoon. The french windows are covered by long, light curtains. One of the front doors is open and a shaft of bright sunlight further lightens the room*

Commander Chittenden (Chitto) enters. He is a good-hearted but not too bright ex-naval officer, who has taken early retirement and is now the local representative for Share-a-Lux Ltd. Portugal's ever-open bars are a source of constant comfort to Chitto, who is permanently well-oiled, but manages to conceal this with extreme dignity and only the occasional slip of the tongue or foot. He carries a briefcase and a clipboard with notepad on it, which he uses extensively. In his pocket he carries a small dictation recorder. He wears a Panama hat and glasses

Chitto walks straight to the telephone as if he knows where it is, lifts the receiver and prepares to dial. His glasses are evidently unsuitable for reading telephone dials. He removes them and puts them aside on the arm of the armchair. He then dials a number and waits, humming contentedly

Chitto (*speaking into the phone*) Ola? Share-a-Lux Timeshare? (*Friendly tone*) Hello there. I want Miss Mogardo per favore ... my secretary ... tck! ... secretario mio ... This is me, dear, Commander Chittenden ... *Chittenden!* (*Raising his voice even more*) No, I know he's not there. I'm here, aren't I?! (*Slowly*) I—wish—to—parler—mit Senorita Mogardo, capisch? (*Pause*) Oh, well done! (*Pause*) Hello, Miss Mogardo. Just reporting in. I'm at L'Aranjina, awaiting the arrival of the first tenants and checking everything's in working order. Then I'll come back to the office. Yes, I've got the tenants' names on my clipboard ... I think ... I hope. Obrigado, Miss Mogardo. (*He hangs up and prepares to move away but his legs have got caught up in the wire which connects to a jack in the wall. In disentangling himself he inadvertently pulls the jack out of its socket. He does not notice this. Then preparing to consult his clipboard he sits on the arm of the armchair and smashes his glasses*) Oh, damn! (*As he gets up to look at the damage he knocks the glasses into the chair. This will enable him to pull out a pre-set pair of obviously wrecked glasses, which he peers at myopically. From now on he acts like Mr Magoo*) Oh, really! What a sorry spectacle! (*He manages to locate a waste basket and drops the glasses into it. He moves back and collides with chair. He peers closely at his clipboard*) Check lights, furnishings, curtains. (*He goes to a light switch, finds it with some difficulty and turns it on. There is a silent flash and a puff of smoke from a wall fitting behind him. He does not see this*) No problems there. (*He then casually straightens a picture on the wall and one next to it falls off the wall*) Oh, dear. (*He tries to re-hang the picture but it won't oblige*) Blasted thing. (*He looks around, then, a trifle furtively, goes to cupboard door, opens it, and places picture inside*) What the eyes don't see ... (*He moves* R *and now searches for a button on the wall* R *of entrance*) Now, electric curtains. (*He finds button, presses it and turns towards window curtains which promptly glide open*) Thank Heaven for that! (*The curtains continue to glide and drop clean off the rail. He looks disconsolate. He gathers up the fallen curtains then, again a bit furtively and hurriedly, crosses to* L *and throws the curtains into the cupboard. He takes a small dictation recorder from his pocket and speaks into it*) Miss Mogardo, please note. Check stops on living-room curtain rail stop. By the way, the last stop is a full stop not a rail stop stop. Obrigado, Miss Mogardo. (*He pockets recorder, thinks*) Check kitchen.

Chitto exits R *into the kitchen colliding with the wall on his way*

Leslie and Eve enter through the front door

Leslie carries two suitcases. He is a diffident man from a modest background. He is wearing a white shirt and looks nervous. Eve is a pretty, self-assured girl. She teeters on high-heeled shoes and her clothes are disturbingly tight. Their clothes are more Costa Brava than Cap d'Antibes. Eve gives Leslie a little shove which propels him further into the room.

Eve Well, go on! It isn't going to bite. (*She looks around*) Oh, this is smashing! Brilliant! (*Dreamily*) And it's all mine for a week every year, for ever. What do you say, Leslie?

Leslie Yes, very nice.

Eve More than nice! (*She touches a piece of furniture*) This isn't rubbish, you know.

Leslie moves L *and opens the bedroom door. He peers inside*

Leslie No, it's very grand. (*He puts a suitcase through the door and closes it*)

Eve Now this is what I call a sofa. (*She sits down*) Ooh! Come and try it.

Leslie (*innocently*) Oh yes.

Leslie sits beside Eve. She immediately lays him flat and starts to kiss him

Steady! Someone might come in.

Eve shuts his mouth with another kiss

Chitto enters from kitchen and stops at the end of sofa but does not see them

Chitto Now, what next?

Eve screams causing Chitto to yell. Eve jumps up and faces Chitto. Leslie sits up

Sorry if I startled you. Didn't hear you come in. I'm Commander Chittenden and how are you, sir?

Chitto extends a hand which Eve takes

Eve I'm not a sir. I'm a madam.

Chitto Good Lord! So sorry. Just broken my specs and I'm blind as a bat without 'em.

Leslie now stands up beside Eve. Chitto dimly takes him in

Ah, and how are you Mister—ah—(*He tries to read clipboard and fails*) sir?

Leslie Very well. (*He points to sofa*) We were just—er—only ...

Eve Never mind, Leslie. (*To Chitto*) I'm very pleased, Commander Chittenden.

Chitto Glad you approve. I can honestly say we are the undisputed leaders in the time-share field. The beauty of Share-a-Lux is that you don't have to be a millionaire to enjoy this. For one week it's all yours and nothing and nobody can take it away from you.

Eve And your company say we are the first people to live here in L'Aranjina?

Chitto Yes, indeed. (*He leans with his hand against the wall*) The paint's hardly dry. (*He notices there is wet paint on his hand. He wipes it off surreptitiously with his handkerchief whilst trying to distract their attention*) Just look at the furnishings. Untouched by human hand. (*He takes out his pocket recorder*) Excuse me. (*To recorder*) Want a quick touch-up.

Eve moves quickly away from Chitto

Eve Pardon?

Chitto No! No! Giving notes to my secretary on this recorder. (*He indicates dictation recorder*) Tremendous gadget if the memory's not too hot.

Eve nods then notices Leslie who is peering nervously out of the window. She moves to him

Eve What are you doing, Leslie?

Leslie Oh, just checking.

Eve What a smashing view!

Chitto Unique, isn't it?

Eve Commander, there don't seem to be any curtains.

Chitto Er—no, you have shutters, louvered shutters. Very handy. You could have curtains, of course, but I don't advise them.

Chitto pulls a shutter into view

Eve Why not?

Chitto Why not? Er—well—they're open weave and the mosquitoes fly straight through them.

Leslie Oh, I see. (*He frowns*) Half a mo. What about all those great gaps in the shutters?

Chitto What about them?

Leslie Won't the mosquitoes fly straight through them as well?

Chitto Not if they're Portuguese.

Leslie The shutters?

Chitto No, the mosquitoes.

Eve (*suspiciously*) What's so special about Portuguese mosquitoes?

Chitto They can't change altitude, y'see, and go up and down—except when mating, but that's another story. So they aim straight for a crack in the slats and stun themselves. (*Quickly as Leslie looks like asking a question*) Now, you'll be wanting to meet your staff. They'll be in their quarters round the back. After you, Mrs Charlesworth.

Eve Thank you, but if you don't mind, the name is Smith.

Chitto (*consulting clipboard*) Are you sure?

Eve Of course I'm sure.

Chitto It certainly looks like Charlesworth to me.

Leslie I expect it's just a typing error.

Eve Charlesworth for Smith! A bloody monkey wouldn't get it that wrong.

Chitto Must be a computer error. Your week is from the tenth to the seventeenth, isn't it?

Eve Yes.

Chitto Splendid! No problem. (*Ushering them out*) This way Mrs Charver ... Charvis ...

Leslie (*as they go*) Smith!

Eve, Leslie and Chitto exit via the balcony

The front door opens and Henry enters followed by Mary

Henry is in his early forties. He is expensively dressed in quality summer clothes—a smart edition of what Leslie is wearing. He keeps a pompous and irascible nature in check most of the time. Mary wears elegant summer clothes. She is good-looking and in her thirties. Both are obviously upper crust

Henry Hello! Charlesworth here. Chittenden! Commander Chittenden! He doesn't seem to be around.

Mary He didn't seem to be at the airport either. I hate unreliability.

Henry Well, you know what they say out here. It's always "Mañana".

Mary No, it isn't. That's Spain. This is Portugal and they should know better.

Henry (*looking around*) Well, what do you think of our little "Time-share by the Sea"?

Mary Super, darling. Rather fun, being the first people to live here.

Henry Great. Shall I bring the luggage in?

Mary No. You've paid for the staff, so let them do it.
Henry Yes, but they don't seem to be around.
Mary (*imperiously*) Staff! Staff!
Henry Darling, they won't understand that.
Mary They will if you shout it loudly enough. Staff! Staff!
Henry As far as I can remember from the phrase book, it's "servidor". (*He calls out*) Servidor! Servidor!
Mary They're obviously not here. (*She shows him a sheet of paper*) The servants' quarters are round the back. Let's dig them out. They're probably snoring their heads off.
Henry Right.

They go through onto the balcony

Servidor!
Mary Staff!
Henry Servidor!
Mary Staff!

Henry and Mary exit from the balcony

Eve and Leslie enter through the front door

Eve I'm boiling. (*She makes for the sofa*) I hope he finds the staff. I'm dying for a drink.
Leslie Can I give you one?
Eve (*cheeky laugh*) Oh, yes please!

Eve pulls Leslie to her

Chitto enters through the front door

Chitto Oh! I do beg your pardon.
Leslie We were only . . . just . . .
Eve All right, Leslie! (*To Chitto*) Any sign of the staff?
Chitto Nowhere about but they'll be along soon. Meanwhile, here is an interesting feature.

Chitto moves up to the drinks trolley and during ensuing speech brings it DC

One of the unique perks you get with Share-a-Lux is a ready-stocked drinks trolley and a hamper of food.
Leslie Now, that's really pushing the boat out.
Chitto And we start with the Share-a-Lux complimentary cocktail.
Eve Ooh, lovely!

Chitto picks up a bottle without a label on it and from it pours two glasses of jet black liquid, which he hands to Eve and Leslie

(*Uncertainly*) Ta.
Chitto No, not tar. It's a prune base, actually.
Leslie Well, that should keep us going.
Eve And have one yourself, Commander.

Chitto Thank you but no. Saw the light two years ago and haven't touched a drop since.

Eve Pity there aren't more like you. Help yourself to a tonic or something, then.

Chitto How very kind. A small gin would be just the tonic I need.

Chitto picks up a tumber which he holds up and then proceeds to fill to the top with gin. Eve and Leslie stare, goggle-eyed

Leslie (*involuntarily*) When!

Chitto Where?

Leslie (*pointing*) There!

Chitto Thanks. Cheers. What do you do for a living, old man?

Leslie I'm in the motor trade.

Chitto Oh, well, never mind. Now if you encounter any problems, you have my number. Just pick up this phone and dial . . . (*He walks to the phone with his glass. He picks up the phone, puts it to his ear and frowns. He jiggles the knobs on the base of the receiver*) Ola! Ola! Ola! Oh dear!

Leslie moves near the phone and points to the floor between the telephone and the wall

Leslie Hasn't the jack come out of the socket in the wall?

Chitto (*peering myopically*) By Jove, you're right! Well spotted. Problem solved.

Chitto gets to his knees, picks up the jack at the end of the cable and approaches the single hole

Well, nearly solved it. Which of these holes does it go into?

Leslie There is only one.

Chitto Really? Looks like two to me. Anyway, I'll take a chance with the one in the middle. (*After a couple of misses, he finds the hole*) Got you! (*He drinks deeply*) That's better. First of the day.

Leslie (*in an undertone*) Glad we weren't here yesterday.

Eve giggles, and digs Leslie in the ribs

Chitto Now for the rest of the royal tour. First the bedrooms. They take the breath away.

Leslie (*close to him*) Promise?

Eve Bedrooms! Now he's talking. Isn't he, Les?

Leslie He seems to be drinking.

Chitto One bedroom has a magnificent antique fourposter, and the other has two singles. Which do you prefer, sir?

Leslie (*confused*) I couldn't say. We've never actually . . .

Chitto Ah! Now I know what's going on.

Leslie No, you don't!

Chitto Yes, I do! You're on your honeymoon. (*He nudges Eve*) Nudge, nudge! Wink, wink!

Eve Clever clogs! Right first time. We'll have the fourposter, won't we, Leslie?

Leslie If you say so.
Chitto You won't regret it. It's the *pièce de ... pièce de ...*
Eve Pieced as a newt.
Leslie Ssssh!
Chitto I'd better give the room a quick tour of inspection. We don't want any nasty surprises. Stay there. I'll be back before you can say Jack—er—Jack—er ...
Leslie Ta.
Chitto Oh, well, he'll do. (*To himself*) Jack Tar?

Chitto exits DL *into the bedroom*

Eve Soon as we get rid of that old soak, we'll give the fourposter a trial run.
Leslie Shouldn't we wait a bit? It's broad daylight. Not even supper time yet.
Eve Where have you been all your life?
Leslie Wakefield.
Eve I meant, haven't you ever played around?
Leslie I'm not a virgin, if that's what you mean, but I've had quite a few rather nasty experiences.
Eve Nasty?
Leslie Well, things are apt to go wrong for me when I ... during—er ...

Eve illustrates his possible failure to rise to the occasion

Eve You mean you can't ... ? It doesn't ... ?
Leslie No! *That's* all right—all things being equal.
Eve So what goes wrong?
Leslie (*shy*) Things. Like I ... well ... we were in this field and there was a cloudburst. Another time a bed-spring sprung out and put me in hospital for a week.

Eve struggles to keep a straight face

Then there was this little dog. (*He taps his rear*) Kept biting me every time I ...
Eve (*laughing as she hugs him*) I think I'm going to find you very refreshing.
Leslie I hope so. I just—worry. When we get back to England, what would happen if I called you "Eve" in front of your husband? I mean, I've only just started calling you "Syd".
Eve I think you're an angel for putting up with the way he treats you.
Leslie I'm not exactly treating him too well right now.
Eve Don't worry. He invented the game, and he never checks on me anyway.
Leslie You've done this before, haven't you?
Eve No. Well, yes. Once.
Leslie That salesman who was there when I first came? Charley?

Eve nods, a bit embarrassed

Whatever happened to him?
Eve Dunno. He disappeared.

Leslie I don't like the sound of that.
Eve Well, not *disappeared* exactly. He just went to ground.
Leslie (*glumly*) Six feet under?
Eve I have sometimes wondered.

There is a crash from the bedroom and a yell of pain from Chitto

What's that? (*She opens the door* DL) He's lying on the floor covered in curtains.

Eve exits DL

Leslie I've got a funny feeling about this holiday.

Leslie exits DL, *closing the door behind him*

Henry enters through the front door

Henry I have an uneasy feeling about this place. It's like the *Marie Celeste*.

Mary enters through the front door

Mary Maybe the staff have sloped off to Mass, or something.
Henry It's too bad. We're going straight down to the office in the village and get some sense out of them. I signed a cast-iron contract and I want it carried out to the letter. Come on.
Mary Can't you forget you're a lawyer for five minutes?
Henry If there's any kind of muddle I'll sue them for damages and misrepresentation.
Mary You'll burst a blood vessel.
Henry Good. I'll sue them for that as well.

Henry and Mary exit through the front door

Eve and Leslie enter DL *from the bedroom*

Leslie That curtain rod could have knocked his brains out.
Eve What's left of them.
Leslie I shudder to think what'll happen if we start bouncing about on that fourposter.

Chitto enters from bedroom DL *carrying a pair of curtains and a rod*

Chitto I do apologize on behalf of the curtains, but I'm told that the maid's husband, Pedro, is a first-class handyman. He'll fix them. In the meantime, I'll just pop them into the—er—curtain cupboard. (*He opens the cupboard door and slings the rods and curtains inside*)
Eve Where are the staff, Commander Chittenden?
Chitto Call me Chitto, please. Everybody does.
Eve Chitto, then. Where are they?
Chitto Should have been here but I'm afraid they may have had trouble with the bus.
Eve Didn't catch it, you mean?
Chitto No, they probably *did*.

Leslie has wandered to the window to take some breaths of air

Leslie It's a huge garden. Is it easy for someone to get in from outside?
Chitto Absolutely. Let me show you. (*He joins Leslie*) Now, you see that gate at the end? That leads to a cliff path which is a short cut to the village.

Chitto leads Leslie onto the balcony

And below the balcony here is your swimming pool.
Leslie Very green water.
Chitto Yes, lovely isn't it?
Eve (*joining them*) Shouldn't it be blue?
Chitto Absolutely! And Pedro will keep it that way. If you want to summon him just ring this bell. (*He picks up a handbell and tinkles it*) And give him his orders.
Eve Does he speak English?
Chitto You may have a problem there. There's very little English spoken in these parts.
Leslie I only know one word: obri ... obrigado; so how do we communicate?
Chitto For a start speak slowly and distinctly as though addressing a toddler or a drunk. (*He puts down his glass*) But this won't get the beds washed, will it? Talking of which I'll just go and make sure everything is tickety-boo in the second bedroom. (*He chuckles*) We don't want any more curtain problems.

Chitto walks straight into the kitchen and straight out again

That, of course is your kitchen. (*He opens the bedroom door* DR) Ah! Bedroom.

Chitto exits DR

Leslie I'd hate to be his liver. (*He looks at the windows*) You know, I'd feel a lot safer if we had curtains in here. I mean, supposing someone sneaked in and spotted us—together?
Eve Who's going to walk in here? There's not a soul around. Now relax and give me a kiss.

Leslie gives Eve a peck on the cheek

I said a kiss.

Eve pulls Leslie down on top of her on the sofa and gives him a passionate kiss. He makes two tentative attempts to put his leg over her thigh. Finally Eve grabs his leg and puts it firmly over her thigh

Leslie (*coming up for air*) Careful!
Eve Now what's the matter?
Leslie Suppose Syd *has* followed you out from England and walks in?
Eve He's not going to follow me, is he? Not after me telling him where I was going.
Leslie Eve, I hate to say this, but if I was Syd and married to you, looking like you do, I don't think I'd believe you'd gone to visit your old geography mistress in a Portuguese nunnery.

Eve Why not? Sister Esperanza *did* teach me, and has moved to a convent in Portugal. So stop being an old worryguts. I'm safely in a nunnery here, and you're touring Wales for Syd, looking for good second-hand cars.

Leslie I still have this nasty empty feeling in my tummy.

Eve That's hunger. I feel peckish, too. See what there is to eat in that hamper.

Leslie goes to the hamper and opens it

Leslie (*reacts*) It's all bottles.

Eve Oh, Gawd! Chitto's struck again!

Leslie (*taking out a bottle*) No. It's not booze.

Eve Must be.

Leslie It's got a picture of a loo on the label.

Eve Get away! It'll be a wine press.

Leslie I never saw a wine press with a cistern and a lavatory chain.

Eve moves over and examines the bottle

Eve Disinfectant! A dozen bottles of disinfectant. That's all we need. What next?

The telephone rings. It has a loud bell. Leslie jumps about a foot in the air

Leslie It's the phone!

Eve Yes.

Leslie It's ringing.

Eve Yes, I can hear it.

Leslie But why?

Eve Somebody's making a call.

Leslie Who?

Eve How should I know? It won't be for us, will it? Probably for Chitto. Answer it, then.

Leslie What shall I say?

Eve Ola.

Leslie Olé?

Eve Ola.

Leslie picks up the phone and puts it to his ear

Leslie (*on the phone*) Olé ... Ola ... (*He freezes*) Oh, Lord!

Leslie stuffs receiver between his legs and is paralysed, incapable of movement or speech. His mouth opens but no sound emerges

Eve What's the matter?

Leslie's voice fails him again

What's up?

Leslie (*at last*) It's him!

Eve Who?

Leslie Syd.

Eve (*moving to him*) You're joking.

Leslie I tell you it's him. I'd know that snarl anywhere.

Leslie still has the receiver wedged between his legs. Eve now pulls it out, causing him considerable renewed pain

Eve (*on the phone*) Hello? . . . Syd, darling! What a lovely surprise? . . . Yes, I got to the nunnery safe and sound . . . What? . . . A man answered the phone? . . . No, that wasn't a man. That was sister Amelia. She teaches unarmed combat . . . Yes, Syd, I know what you'd do if ever I cheated on you.

Leslie nearly faints

But I wouldn't in a nunnery, would I? Sister Esperanza sends her love. She's here beside me. We're just going in to Vespers.

Leslie seizes the little handbell and rings it frantically, at the same time starting to sing a Gregorian chant dreadfully off-key, and finishing with a very long "Amen". He starts again, marching round

(*To Leslie*) Oh, shut up! . . . No, not you, Syd. By the way, how on earth did you get the convent number? . . . I left it on a pad? . . . (*She mouths something unrepeatable*) Of course I did. On purpose, for you, in case of emergencies. I must have forgot to tell you. So what do you want, Syd? . . . You're *checking*?

Leslie groans audibly

(*Waving angrily at Leslie*) Checking on what, Syd? . . . Oh, to see if it was the right number. Well, it is. Look, lover, I have to go now. They'll be sounding the last bell.

Leslie loudly rings the bell, which flies out of his hand

And there it goes. Good-bye darling. Thanks for calling. (*She hangs up and grimaces*) Whew!

Leslie I knew it. I knew something would go wrong.

Eve It'll be okay if we keep our wits about us.

Leslie And where was he phoning from, may I ask?

Eve The showroom, I suppose.

Leslie You *suppose*. He could be in a phone box round the corner, waiting to pounce. I'm going to find out.

Leslie moves to the phone and picks up a booklet with dialling codes. He leafs through it

England . . . Great Britain . . . four-seven-two-two.

Eve What are you doing?

Leslie I'm going to ring him at the office. That way at least I'll know if he's there. (*He starts to dial*)

Eve You're mad. He'll recognize your voice.

Leslie Of course he will. I'm going to tell him I'm in Wales.

Eve You'll muck it up.

Leslie Sssh! (*He cups his hand over the phone*) It's him. (*He uncups the phone and adopts an appalling Welsh accent*) 'Ullo! 'Ullo! May I speak to Sydney Travis of Mile End Motors ... Oh it's himself indeed to goodness ... Well, this is the Three Leaks Hotel whateffer and there's a feller in room thirteen who is after talking to you begorrah. Hold on. (*He pauses*)

Eve (*hissing at Leslie*) Begorrah! That's Irish, you twit.

Leslie Sssh! (*Into the phone, in his own voice*) Hello, Syd? Is that you? This is me. Leslie ... Leslie Boothroyd ... Yes, that berk ... Just thought you'd like to know that I'm safely in Wales ... Whereabouts in Wales? (*This temperarily stumps him*) Er—um ... er ... in ... er ...

Eve (*hissing*) Prestatyn.

Leslie (*panicking*) Press what in?

Eve grabs the phone from him and speaks into it in a sort of Welsh accent

Eve I'm sorry caller your time is up. (*She slams the phone down*) Idiot!

Leslie Never mind. I feel better.

There is a crash and a cry from Chitto offstage in the bedroom DR

Eve Oh, Gawd! Chitto doesn't.

Chitto, draped in a pair of curtains and carrying a rod, enters DR

Leslie obligingly opens the cupboard door for him

Leslie This way, sir.

Chitto Good job I checked.

Eve I'm beginning to see why we have a curtain cupboard.

Chitto Yes, very useful. (*He throws the curtains into the cupboard and closes the door*)

Leslie Commander, how would you say: "This is the Convent of Santa Maria" on the telephone?

Chitto I'd say ... (*He thinks hard*) ... I'd say: "This is the Convent of Santa Maria".

Leslie No, I meant how would you say it in Portuguese?

Chitto In Portuguese? Oh. (*He thinks again*) Well, I'd probably say: "Ola, this is the Convent of Santa Maria".

Eve (*sarcastically*) Thanks very much. Now, are you well enough to hear about another cock-up?

Chitto Depends. What would that be?

Eve You said there was a food hamper.

Chitto Mouthwatering. I check every item myself. One of the many surprises you get when you open it ...

Eve Is a dozen bottles of disinfectant.

Chitto picks up a bottle and examines it

Chitto This is ridiculous! You can't be expected to eat disinfectant. One can barely drink the stuff except in dire emergencies. (*He puts the disinfectant in the pocket of his jacket*)

Leslie Never mind. We'll go down to the village and stock-up.

Chitto Good grief! You want more? You won't get through a dozen bottles in a week.

Eve He was talking about *food*. You know, the hamper.

Chitto The food, yes. And if you get thirsty down there there's the Castello bar, the one opposite or the one round the corner. My car's here so if you'd like me to drive you . . .

Eve No, thanks.

Chitto No, probably less dangerous if you take the cliff path. Lovely view but a mugger's paradise.

Eve (*sarcastically*) Thanks for telling us!

Leslie (*ever nervous*) What is it like for burglars round here?

Chitto (*enthusiastic*) Tremendous.

Eve Thanks again, Commander!

Chitto Chitto, please, Mrs Charlesworth.

Eve *Smith*!

Chitto Yes, yes, of course. I'm so sorry. How stupid of me. I know it's a frightful cheek but names are not my strong suit. Would you object terribly if I called you Charlesworth from time to time?

Eve Yes, I would.

Eve walks away irritably. Leslie moves to where she has been standing. Chitto rubs his eyes as if suffering from a bad headache

Chitto Say no more. Charlesworth it shall not be. (*To Leslie*) I'm extremely sorry Mrs Smith. I'm not usually as addlepated as this.

Leslie Good. Because I'm not Mrs Smith.

Chitto Oh, God! Now I'm seeing things. Between you, me and the gatepost that last curtain rod cracked me on the head. I was wondering if I might stay and have ten minutes shut-eye?

Leslie looks at Eve, who nods

Leslie Sure. Help yourself.

Chitto How very kind.

Chitto heads straight for the bar to pour himself a drink. Leslie stops him

Leslie Excuse me. I meant feel free to use the sofa or the spare bed for a few minutes.

Leslie moves the drinks trolley back to its original position

Chitto Most thoughtful.

Leslie and Eve move towards the french windows

Leslie (*to Chitto*) Oh, is there a chemist in the village?

Chitto Yes, next door to the Castello bar.

Leslie Good. (*To Eve*) There's something I forgot to bring.

Eve There's no problem. I'm on the Pill.

Leslie But are they any good for a sore throat?

Eve and Leslie exit via the balcony

Chitto takes out his tape recorder and speaks into it

Chitto Miss Mogardo. When I bump into you, say: "Charlesworth and disinfectant," or "Smith and disinfectant". I can't remember which or why.

Chitto exits into the bedroom DR *and closes the door*

Henry and Mary enter through the front door

Henry Commander Chittenden? Commander Chittenden?

Mary That Share-a-Lux woman, Miss Mogadon or whatever she's called, said he's bound to show up here any moment, so for Heaven's sake do calm down.

Henry Yes, you're right. No point in upsetting oneself. (*He sinks into the sofa with a sigh*) Ah, that's better.

Mary Henry, that sofa worries me.

Henry What's the matter with it?

Mary It's facing the wrong way for the view. Help me switch it round with the chair.

Henry helps Mary to change the position of sofa and chair

Henry Why do women always want to shift furniture around?

Mary We only do when it's in the wrong place.

Henry They probably shoved it down when they delivered it. We're the first owners, remember.

Mary (*adjusting the position of a chair*) There! That's better.

Henry Got to admit it. It *is* an improvement.

Mary moves to the window and goes onto the balcony

Mary Here's something I couldn't even try to improve—the view.

Henry joins her on the balcony

Henry Not bad. Not bad at all. (*He chuckles*) Ah, well, that's one question answered.

Mary What?

Henry (*pointing*) They do go topless in Portugal.

Mary (*slapping his arm down*) Henry!

Henry Ouch! (*He rubs his tummy*) Careful. You nearly ruined our holiday.

Mary Like you ruined it last year in Cannes.

Henry Oh, not that old song again! For the last time, I never touched the girl. I was helping her look for her contact lens.

Mary Down her front?

Henry Well, it wouldn't be down her back, would it?

Mary There are other things to look at apart from bare tops.

Henry Yes, but very few countries allow the full frontal on their beaches.

Mary Sometimes I despair of you. You behave more like a smutty schoolboy than a successful barrister.

Henry (*teasing*) Sorry, my dear. I promise I won't make any more boobs. (*He pats her bottom*) And you can make me a cup of tea.

Mary If there is any tea. I'll put the kettle on.
Henry Super.
Mary But I must freshen up first. (*She opens the door* DR) Bedroom. Got it in one.

Mary exits

Henry gallops straight back to look out over the balcony. If it is considered best he could have a pair of binoculars. He gives a whoop of joy at what he sees

Henry By George! Good old Portugal! It *is* one of those beaches.

He jumps guiltily and hides binoculars at the sound of a shrill scream from Mary DR

Mary enters DR

Mary There's a man with his trousers off.
Henry No, it's a woman with her bottoms off.
Mary There's a man in the bedroom taking his trousers off.
Henry What!

Chitto enters DR *doing up his trousers. He peers at them myopically*

Chitto Putting 'em on, actually. (*He goes to Henry*) Sorry if I gave you a shock, my dear young lady.
Henry Young *lady*?

It should be noted that in the early part of this scene Chitto and Mary are not in close proximity so that she is out of what eyeline he possesses

Chitto (*reacting*) A thousand apologies Mr—er—old chap. But what with no specs and that crack on the nut I can't seem to focus.
Henry Obviously.
Chitto I mean how could I have mistaken you for your big, beautiful and, if I may say so, buxom wife?

Mary creeps up and stands right behind Henry

Henry May he say it, darling?
Mary (*hissing*) Who is he?

Henry shrugs

Chitto You two are back very quickly.
Henry Back?
Chitto Did you find it?
Henry Find what?
Chitto The bar.
Henry What bar?
Chitto The Castello Bar, the one opposite or the one round the corner.
Mary We haven't been to any bar.

Chitto sees her for the first time

Chitto Oh, hello again (*He reacts*) You look shorter. You're not wearing high heels any more.

Henry I don't know who you think you are ...

Chitto Oh, I know who I am. Chittenden. Got that straight, and you'll be happy to know that I have the name question completely buttoned up. (*Triumphant*) You are Leslie and Eve Smith.

Henry Charlesworth.

Chitto What!

Mary Henry and Mary Charlesworth.

Chitto Haven't we been through all this? (*He squints at clipboard*) And anyway, Charlesworth's nothing like Smith.

Henry Why should it be?

Chitto Because you kept insisting your name was Smith. (*He indicates Mary*) Eve here will bear me out.

Mary Someone should. Eve?

Henry You did say you were Commander Chittenden?

Chitto Yes. You're spot on. I do admire you chaps who can remember names.

Henry I wish you would remember ours.

Chitto squints myopically at the clipboard

Chitto I did but they seem to have been crossed out. Anyway, welcome to L'Aranjina.

Mary Thank you, Commander.

Chitto Chitto, please.

Mary Thank you. It looks extremely nice. And we are the first people to move in, aren't we?

Chitto Yes. (*He frowns*) Didn't I tell you that just now?

Mary No.

Chitto Odd. (*He sighs*) I had hoped that last spell in hospital had done the trick.

Mary We were expecting a couple who would be looking after us.

Chitto Pedro and Maria. They still not here?

Henry No.

Chitto Ah well. They live in the next village. I hear they're splendid workers.

Henry You say you "hear" they're good. Don't you vet the staff yourself?

Chitto Yes, but in this case, no, because I've only recently come out.

Henry (*sympathetically*) How long did they keep you in?

Chitto No, from head office, out from England to work here in—in—er— er—(*He snaps his fingers*) Go down to Spain and turn sharp right.

Mary (*raised eyebrows*) Portugal!

Chitto Well done!

Henry and Mary exchange a helpless look

Mary Anyway, about this couple we're expecting ...

Chitto (*chattily*) Yes, do tell me about them.

Henry The *servants*! Pedro and Maria!

Chitto Ah! Yes. I'm sorry. They're not here but she keeps on breaking down.

Mary Maria?

Chitto No. The bus—a real old crock and often doesn't get up the mountain road. And you'll be glad to know, Maria's a first class cook and Pedro'll put his hand to anything.

Henry Let's hope he puts it to the bus.

Mary Do they speak English?

Chitto Are you sure we've not been through all this before?

Mary How could we since we've never met?

Chitto That's a very good question.

Mary So, do they speak English?

Chitto Ah, well. (*He takes a deep breath*) Here goes. Talk to them very slowly as if addressing a toddler or a drunk; which reminds me, where are my manners? You must be parched. (*He moves up to the trolley*) One of the perks of Share-a-Lux is a well-stocked drinks trolley and a hamper of disinfectant. So what's your poison?

Mary and Henry exchange helpless looks. Chitto notices the two black cocktails previously poured out and untouched by Leslie and Eve

But I forgot—your Share-a-Lux complimentary cocktails!

Chitto picks up the glasses and proffers them

Mary (*shuddering*) Ugh!

Henry We don't care for cocktails, thank you.

Mary And certainly not that one.

Henry But don't let us stop you.

Chitto Oh, no thanks. Took the pledge years ago.

Henry Wise man. Have a soft drink, then.

Chitto How very kind. I'll just sample a drop of gin, if that's all right with you.

Henry Oh. For a moment I thought you were a teetotaller.

Chitto Not totally. (*He dispenses his own drink*) Your astonishing health. (*He drinks deeply*)

Henry Cheers.

Chitto Ah! First of the day. So how are things back home in the old motor trade?

Henry (*coldly*) I work at the Bar.

Chitto (*immediately interested*) Oh? Wonder if I know it. Which one?

Henry (*giving up*) I'll get the luggage in.

Henry exits through front door

Chitto looks at Mary, puzzled. His next words roughly describe Eve's clothes

Chitto You don't ever wear pink shorts, do you?

Mary Sometimes. Why?

Chitto (*pleased*) Oh, splendid! Like in here ten minutes ago.

Mary No. Unlike you, I don't strip off in public.
Chitto Very worrying. It's definitely broken down.
Mary The bus?
Chitto No. The old brainbox.

The telephone rings. Chitto picks it up

   (*On the phone*) Ola? . . . What? . . . Who? . . . Where? . . . Just a minute. (*He cups the phone, turns to Mary*) Are you by any remote chance a nun called Sister Esperanza?
Mary No, I am not.
Chitto Someone called Syd seems to think you are.
Mary And I wouldn't know anybody called Syd.
Chitto Strange fellow. He called me Sister Amelia. (*Into the phone*) Sorry, old chap, wrong number.

Henry, with cases, enters through front door

Henry Which is the master suite?
Chitto Good Lord! How remiss of me! Still haven't shown you around, have I? You'll find there's nothing lacking. (*He moves to cupboard door*) This, for example, is your—er—you won't find many of these.
Mary What is it?

Chitto opens the cupboard door

Chitto (*remembering*) Oh. It's your—er—curtain cupboard.
Henry Why keep curtains in a cupboard?
Chitto Well, you don't want to leave them hanging around, do you?
Henry (*changing the subject deliberately*) Just show us the master suite.
Chitto Depends on what you fancy—sea view or mountain view.
Mary Definitely sea view.
Chitto (*pointing* R) Starboard side.
Mary Thank you. Now we would like to be on our own for a bit.
Chitto For a bit . . . ? Ah! Of course! Your honeymoon!
Mary ⎫ (*together*) Honeymoon?
Henry ⎭
Chitto Clean forgot. Message received and understood. Nudge, nudge! Wink, wink! I shall now make myself scarce. Cheerio!

Chitto walks firmly into the cupboard and closes the door behind him. Mary and Henry look at one another in astonishment. A pause. The cupboard door opens and Chitto looks out

   May I come in? (*He comes out without his clipboard*) Just checking the curtains. All present and correct. (*He moves, stops, pats his pockets*) Now what did I do with my thingummyjig?
Henry (*losing patience*) Commander, can you find your own way out?
Chitto I shall most certainly try. Generally do in the end.

Henry and Mary move DR *with their cases. Henry catches a glimpse of Chitto as he marches firmly into the cupboard again*

Henry My God! He's done it again!

Henry and Mary exit DR

Chitto emerges from cupboard waving his clipboard

Chitto Found it! Mr Smith? Leslie? Oh, to hell with it. Time for a snifter.

Chitto takes out bottle of disinfectant from his pocket and has a good swig before he exits through front door

Leslie and Eve enter on the balcony and come into the room. They both carry plastic shopping bags. Items which may be seen are a bottle of wine and a bottle of champagne and a French loaf

Eve (*taking Leslie's bag*) I'll bung this stuff in the kitchen and shove the champagne in the freezer. We'll drink it in bed. (*She points*) Or lying on that rug.

Eve exits into the kitchen

Leslie On a rug! In broad daylight! Well, I suppose it's better than behind a bike shed in Wakefield. (*He feels the floor*) Blimey! Hard as a rock. (*He sits on the sofa*)

Eve (*off*) I'm warming up the chicken but we forgot to buy Nescaff.

Leslie Never mind. I'd as soon have tea. In fact, I'd rather have tea than almost anything.

Eve enters from the kitchen. She has put on an apron

Eve Oh, thanks! This'll be a riot of a holiday.

Leslie I meant before.

Eve Before we make love?

Leslie No, before the champagne.

Eve Thanks again, Sir Galahad. (*Looking puzzled*) Here, did you just muck around with the furniture?

Leslie What do you mean?

Eve I'll swear this sofa was facing the other way, and that chair.

Leslie You're right. They were. I thought there was something different about the room.

Eve Must have been done while we were down in the village.

Leslie Who by?

Eve Who do you think? Chitto, of course.

Leslie Why should he move our furniture about?

Eve Probably collided with it!

Leslie Unless it's the staff.

Eve Could be, I suppose, but if Pedro and Maria have arrived, where are they?

Leslie They'll be around somewhere. Unpacking perhaps.

Eve Help me put the furniture back.

Leslie I wouldn't bother.

Eve I would. I won't have them taking charge of us. Come on.

Leslie rolls up his sleeves. They begin shifting sofa and chair back to their original positions

Leslie You don't think they'll be offended?
Eve I don't give a monkey's if they are. This is my house for the week. That's better. You have to let these foreigners know who's boss, or you find they're running your lives.

Henry and Mary enter through archway DR. *They are now casually dressed. They see Leslie in white shirt with rolled up sleeves and Eve in an apron*

Mary Oh!
Henry Ah!

Both couples now automatically assume that the other couple is Pedro and Maria. As instructed, they all speak slowly and distinctly and with a lot of smiles

Leslie Ah!
Eve Oh!
Mary (*looking at Eve*) Maria!
Eve (*nods*) Maria.
Henry (*to Leslie*) Pedro.
Leslie (*nods*) Pedro.
Mary Ola?
Eve Ola!
Henry Ola!
Leslie Ola!
Mary Bom dia!
Eve Bom dia!
Henry Bom dia!
Leslie Bom dia!
Mary (*pointing to window*) Boa vista.
Eve Si! Boa vista.
Mary Mucho sol!
Henry MUCHO SOL. Mucho burno, sol?
Leslie (*gaining confidence*) Ah, si! Mucho sol, mucho burno! ... Oucho!
Henry Vous very welcomos.
Leslie Grazias!
Mary Obrigado!
Leslie Obrigado!
Henry Obrigado!
Eve Obrigado!

Mary looks towards the kitchen then turns to Eve

Mary Vous preparos mangare in cuccina?
Eve Si. Pollow in cuccina.
Mary Pollow?

Eve clucks like a chicken and flaps arms like wings

Ah! Pollyo!

Eve Si! Pollyo rosto.

Henry and Leslie both mime clucking chickens

Mary Superbo! (*She rubs tummy*) Yum! Yum! Hungaro.
Eve Si!
Henry Si! Obrigado!
Leslie Obrigado!
Mary Obrigado!
Eve Obrigado!

Henry and Mary start to move towards the kitchen when Mary notices the furniture has been moved. She nudges Henry and points. They exchange an almost Laurel-and-Hardy nod then, after a hard glance at Leslie and Eve, they change the position of the sofa and chair to the way they like it

Henry Voila!
Mary Este es correctos por nostros.
Eve Oh, si?
Mary Adios!
Henry Arrivaderchey.
Eve Obrigado!
Mary De nada.
Leslie Granada!

Mary and Henry exit into the kitchen, closing the door

Eve Granada! Honestly!
Leslie I thought I'd try something different instead of just copying what they said.
Eve That's Spanish, anyway.
Leslie Oh; but they didn't seem to mind.
Eve Amazing isn't it. Quite a lot of words are almost the same.
Leslie Yeah!
Eve I mean in English and Portuguese. I understood far more than I thought I would.
Leslie And they don't seem too bad, do they?
Eve Barring one little item, which still has to be sorted out.
Leslie What's that?
Eve This furniture.
Leslie Oh look, do you think we should?
Eve Yes! (*She moves to the furniture*) Reverse the positions. S'pose we marched into their little cottage and, right in front of them, switched their furniture around. How do you think they'd react?
Leslie Yes, I suppose they'd be very narked.
Eve Exactly—and this is *my* house.

They again switch sofa and chair to their liking

Leslie (*as they push*) So long as we keep on the right side of them, that's all.
Eve (*as they push*) Stop being so humble. Dinner's nearly ready—I've done most of it.

Leslie I wonder if she'd make me some chips? I suddenly fancy chips.

Henry comes out of the kitchen evidently in search of something. He stops dead as he sees Leslie and Eve completing the move

Leslie Correctos for ussos.

Henry almost speaks then turns and re-enters the kitchen

Eve One nil to the home team. See? He didn't argue.
Leslie He didn't smile either.

Mary and Henry enter from the kitchen

They march to the sofa, on which Leslie and Eve are now seated, and solemnly change the position again. Mary whistles loudly and aggressively as she works. Henry whistles on a lower key

Mary and Henry exit into the kitchen, closing the door firmly

Eve Right. This is war.
Leslie Go easy now, Eve.

They begin to move the furniture back to its former position

Eve Go easy! I'll show them.
Leslie Don't let a little thing like this spoil our holiday.
Eve For the umpteenth time—this is my house!
Leslie I know, but if you start shouting they could just walk out.
Eve Good! They're a frosty looking pair of goons, anyway.

The furniture is now re-arranged

Crunch time.
Leslie Wait! Don't do anything rash. I read somewhere that the Portuguese have a vicious streak, slit your throat as soon as look at you.
Eve Sit down on that chair.
Leslie Why?
Eve Just sit.
Leslie What for?
Eve *Sit*! Now stay!

Leslie sits as commanded

Eve goes to the kitchen door, throws it open and yells

OY !!!

Eve then runs back and lies full length on the sofa. She starts to whistle

Henry and Mary enter from the kitchen. Mary has a large carving knife in her hand. Henry is armed with a pair of secateurs

They walk grimly towards the sofa and chair. Mary approaches Leslie with the knife threateningly near him. Leslie takes an apple from the bowl on the table next to him, then grabs the knife from Mary and starts to peel the apple

Leslie Obrigado!

Mary signals to Henry with a jerk of the head. They turn and march back into the kitchen, closing the door

Eve relaxes, stands up

Leslie Did you see the way she came at me with that knife?
Eve Didn't use it, did she?
Leslie What about the look in her eye?
Eve The main thing is they backed off.
Leslie For the time being.
Eve Go and have a listen at the door. If they're plotting something we may find out what it is.
Leslie But they'd be plotting in Portuguese.
Eve Yes, they would, sly brutes. Have a squint through the keyhole, then see what they're cooking up.

Leslie nervously approaches the kitchen door and peeks through the keyhole. He utters a gasp, turns to Eve

Leslie It's our chicken they're cooking up and what's more they're going to eat it.
Eve That does it! They're out on their ear *now*.
Leslie No. Just get hold of that Commander and he'll get rid of them. He said to do that, didn't he?
Eve I suppose so. Where did he say we could find him?
Leslie The Castello Bar, the one opposite or the one round the corner.

Eve quietly pushes the bolt on the kitchen door home

What are you doing?
Eve Bolting the door.
Leslie What's the use of that? They'll just climb out the window.
Eve No, they won't. It's barred.
Leslie You don't think it's going too far, locking them up?
Eve Too far? You know what my Syd would do to anyone who nicked his property?
Leslie No, what?
Eve Break their arms.
Leslie (*as they go*) I wish I hadn't asked.

Eve and Leslie exit via the balcony

The kitchen door is rattled

Henry (*off*) Pedro! Maria!
Mary (*off*) It's locked!

Chitto enters through front door. He carries clipboard

Chitto Ahoy, there, honeymooners! May I come aboard?
Henry (*off*) Open the door!

Henry evidently begins to kick violently at the kitchen door. Chitto goes to the kitchen door and tries it

Chitto It's locked.
Henry (*off*) Of course it's locked. Un-bloody-lock it!

Chitto locates the bolt and slides it back. He stands back upstage of the door

Chitto Try it now.

The door flies open and obviously flattens Chitto behind it

Henry and Mary come out of the kitchen and close the door

They are in time to see Chitto slump down to the ground. They kneel down and half lift Chitto up

Henry I'm most terribly sorry, old man.
Chitto What about?
Henry What I did to you.
Chitto What did you do to me?
Henry You don't remember?
Chitto No. I'd remember if I did, I think.
Henry In that case, let's forget it.

They help Chitto onto the sofa

Chitto I have and it's jolly decent of you, if I may say so.

Chitto now slides off sofa to sit on the floor

Mary Are you quite compos again now?
Chitto Never better. Why?
Mary I have to tell you, I have a serious complaint.
Chitto Well, there's a lot of it about.
Mary A lot of what?
Chitto It's the water. That's why I never touch the stuff.
Mary That is not what I meant. I wish to complain about the servants.
Chitto Oh, they've arrived, have they?
Mary Yes, and they're running wild.
Henry For a start they keep shifting the furniture.
Chitto Excuse me, but would you mind terribly if I sat down?
Henry By all means.

Henry helps Chitto into the armchair

Chitto It's rather uncomfortable on the floor. Did I fall over, by any chance?
Henry Um—yes.
Chitto Thought so. I do sometimes. Between you, me and the—er—gatepost I have a slight weakness.
Henry Yes, we had noticed.
Chitto Had you? Observant of you. It's the ankle. Now, Madam, about your gyppy tummy ...

Mary Commander, I have *not* got a gyppy tummy.
Chitto No? Thought you said it was running wild.
Eve (*losing patience*) Commander Chittenden . . . !
Chitto *Chitto*, please!
Mary I must talk to you about Pedro and Maria.
Chitto Pleasant couple I'm told.
Henry You're wrong—they're totally insane.
Mary They locked us up in the kitchen and have marched off somewhere.
Henry Probably with our valuables. Reminds me, I'd better check.

Henry exits DR

Chitto Well, this is very cosy! What were we talking about?
Mary Pedro and Maria. What do you know about them?
Chitto Not much, but they come highly recommended by a client in our first development—Colonel Wagstaff.

Henry enters DR

Henry Nothing missing. Excuse me a sec, I'm famished.

Henry exits to the kitchen

Mary Could you arrange for me to have a word with this Colonel Wagstaff?
Chitto That could be rather difficult.
Mary Why?
Chitto He's dead.
Mary Oh!
Chitto Poisoned.
Mary Poisoned?
Chitto Food. Strange business.
Mary Foul play?
Chitto (*slight chuckle*) Sort of. He ate a foul chicken. (*More serious*) Must have been seriously contaminated. Pedro and Maria were devastated.
Mary You mean Pedro and Maria cooked it?
Chitto Yes, but oddly enough they didn't eat it.
Mary Oh, my God!

Henry enters from the kitchen chewing on a chicken leg

Henry, Henry, we're in mortal danger, possibly dying.
Henry Have you lost your marbles?
Mary Those crazy servants murdered their last employer.
Henry What! How?
Mary *With a poisoned chicken!*

Henry stares at the chicken leg, his knees sag and he clutches his throat

Henry (*hoarsely*) Poisoned chicken! I thought it tasted funny.
Mary Of course it tasted funny! It's probably laced with cyanide.

Henry groans and chokes

They are killers. We must get a doctor.

Mary goes to the telephone and jiggles the armrest. Henry continues to cough and wheeze and goes purple in the face. Mary bangs down the receiver

Dead!

Chitto Yes. He ate the poisoned chicken.

Mary The *phone* is dead!

Chitto Told you that, didn't I? Or did I? Anyway, it'll be on again in the morning.

Mary We could be dead by morning.

Chitto (*philosophically*) Well, that's life, isn't it. (*To Henry*) You should have that cough seen to.

Mary How soon after he ate the chicken did this Colonel Wagstaff die?

Chitto Instantaneous, Keeled over like a drunk.

Mary (*slightly mollified*) Well, at least that hasn't happened to us. (*To Henry*) How do you feel darling?

Henry All right, I think. You had some, too, how do you feel?

Mary All right, I think, but there's no point in taking chances. We should see a doctor anyway. Where do we find him?

Chitto The Castello Bar, the one opposite or the one round the corner. Between you, me and the—er—the—er (*he points*) that thing out there with the gate on it, he's a bit of a boozer.

Henry Oh, God! He would be!

Mary Just our luck.

Chitto I'll drive you down.

Mary Are you all right to drive?

Chitto Funny you should ask that. I tried to convince the local police chief the other day after I'd had a little contretemps with a donkey.

Mary What was his reaction?

Chitto Brayed loudly and kicked the bumper off. Shall we go?

Henry No, we have our own hired car. We'll find the doctor. By the way what's his name?

Chitto Dunno. One of these impossible Portuguese names. But you can't miss him. He's stone deaf.

Mary How on earth do you recognize a stone deaf doctor?

Chitto That's simple. Go into all the bars, shout "Medico" loud as you can and see who doesn't turn round.

Mary We'll be back shortly. Wait for us.

Henry and Mary go to the front door and exit

Chitto Roger Willco. (*Thoughtfully*) Or was it Robert Willco? Tall chap. Big nose. (*He spots the fact that the jack of the telephone is out of the wall*) Phone isn't dead at all; just come out of the wall, (*He aims jack at wall*) keep still you little ... Gotcha!

Leslie enters through french windows carrying one of Eve's shoes which has lost its heel

Leslie Oh there you are. We've been looking for you.

Chitto I say, you're back very quickly (*he indicates the front door*) and I could have sworn you and your wife went out that way.

Leslie We fell down on the cliff path. My wife caught her heel in a hole and she's broken it

Chitto What rotten luck; but a good thing you were on your way to the doctor.

Leslie Doctor?

Chitto About the chicken.

Leslie Chicken? And why would we want the doctor?

Chitto To set her broken ankle.

Leslie (*laughs*) No! It's only a little sprain; but the most urgent thing to deal with is the cobblers.

Chitto What!

Leslie Cobblers.

Chitto (*wincing*) My dear old chap, I *am* sorry. Bad news for both of you.

Leslie Yes, they're her favourite pair.

Chitto (*a little embarrassed*) Yes, no doubt.

Leslie He'd still be at work at this hour, would he?

Chitto Oh, naturally, but I must warn you he's a bit heavy-handed.

Leslie Oh?

Chitto And, at this hour, they tend to shake a bit, too.

Leslie Well, he can always use a vice.

Chitto (*shudders*) Don't even mention such a thing. Oh, and just remember I warned you he was deaf.

Leslie No, you didn't but, anyway, how does deafness affect cobblers?

Chitto He won't hear you if his grip becomes too much and you suddenly yell: "LET GO"!

Leslie I can't see what all the fuss is about. All he has to do is lay it on the table and give it one clout with a hammer.

Chitto (*holding up a hand*) Rather not pursue the matter. Do you mind?

Leslie Now listen, you, that Pedro and Maria are a pain in the neck and they're probably dangerous. Now we want you to get rid of them.

Chitto Robert Willco.

Leslie We've locked them in here ... (*He moves to the kitchen door and sees the bolt has been drawn. He opens the door and looks through*) Did you open this door?

Chitto No, you did, just then. I saw you with my own eyes.

Eve enters through the french windows wearing one shoe and limping

Eve You've been a long time. I got tired of waiting.

Leslie Sorry, I got delayed. How's the ankle?

Eve I've got a blister now.

Leslie I'll find a plaster.

Leslie exits into the bedroom DL

Chitto Don't upset yourself. I'll go and get Doctor Whatsisname, Mrs Charlesworth.

Eve (*wearily*) Smith.

Chitto That doesn't sound like a Portuguese doctor.
Eve I don't need a doctor, anyway. I'll just shove on a plaster.
Chitto I'm more concerned about your husband's problem.
Eve (*guilty start*) My husband? Has he phoned?
Chitto Phoned?
Eve (*recovering*) Oh, my husband! There's nothing wrong with him. He just slipped on his bum.
Chitto Rather more than that. He obviously doesn't want to worry you but he came out of it rather badly.
Eve No! He just slid down and laughed.
Chitto Through tears. I know the pain.
Leslie (*off*) Eve! Found a plaster.
Eve Coming.

Eve exits DL

The phone rings. Chitto picks it up

Chitto Ola? . . . What? . . . Speak up. It's a very bad line . . . No, I'm not Sister Esperanza . . . Pardon? . . . What is a monk doing in a nunnery? I'm sorry I don't like dirty jokes. (*He slams down the telephone*)

Leslie and Eve enter DL

Leslie We've got her plastered all right now.
Chitto Go easy. Always advisable for one of you to stay sober. Well, I'll slip off and get the doc. Unless it's treated fast this could put paid to your honeymoon and future prospects.
Eve Oh, cobblers!
Chitto Ah! Then he did tell you.

Chitto exits through the front door

Leslie Can you understand a word that man says?
Eve Don't even try. Chitto is blotto. (*She notices the open kitchen door and looks in*) Hey! What happened to Pedro and Maria?
Leslie Escaped.
Eve How?
Leslie Either they're Houdinis or that idiot let them out.
Eve Didn't you ask him?
Leslie You ever tried asking him anything? His brain's gone walkabout.
Eve They've been at the furniture again. Give me a hand.
Leslie Don't start that again.
Eve Come on, push.

Henry and Mary enter through the front door as Eve and Leslie start to move sofa and chair

Mary (*thunderous*) HALTOS IMMEDIATIOS!
Eve Como?
Henry Attenzio uno momento, mis amigos.
Mary Scusi!

Mary starts to move the chair. Leslie delivers a gentle smack on her wrists

Leslie Stoppo! Non moovari furnituros!

Henry gives Leslie a belligerent push

Henry Non molestos mi feminos!

Leslie starts to lose his temper for the first time. He clenches a fist

Leslie Non touchos meos!
Henry Put 'em uppos!
Leslie Rightos!
Eve Go on, Les! Kill him!
Leslie I will, I will.
Mary Biff him one, Henry.

Henry and Leslie square up then suddenly the penny drops with all four of them

Leslie Biff him one? You speaka de Inglees?
Henry Vy not? Vee ees Englees! Why *you* speaka da English?
Leslie Because we are English.
Henry We thought you were Pedro and Maria.
Leslie Snap!
Henry We're all English! (*He laughs*)
Eve And to think you two nearly hit each other in Portugoose!
Mary And we thought you'd poisoned us with the chicken.
Henry Ha! Yes!
Mary Just goes to show how easily wars break out.

General laughter and back slapping

Henry (*with an arm round Eve*) We'll make a little peace, shall we? (*To Leslie*) And a very choice little piece, too, if I may say so.

Mary shoots him a look

No, I may not.
Leslie (*vastly relieved*) What a relief! (*To Mary*) I nearly died when you came at me with that knife.
Mary It was purely in self defence.

Leslie laughs, gaining confidence by the minute

Leslie I reckon a few introductions are in order. Come on Pedro, what's your real name?
Henry Henry. Henry Charlesworth.
Leslie (*roaring with laughter*) Charlesworth! Yes, it would be!
Henry What's so funny?
Leslie You've met old Chitto?
Henry Yes.
Leslie When we first arrived he kept calling us Charlesworth. Anyway, I'm pleased to meet you. I'm Leslie—er—Smith and this is my—er—wife, Eve.

Henry How do you do, Eve. And this is my wife, Mary.
Eve Not so far off Maria, then!

Eve gives Mary a friendly push. Mary contents herself with a cool smile

Mary No, but I hardly think I look like a maid!
Eve What, might I ask, are you doing in our house?
Mary *Your* house?
Eve Well, obviously there's some explanation.
Henry There most certainly is.
Leslie Has to be! You don't look like squatters!
Henry The explanation, Smith, is that this is our house, for the week.
Eve Not for the second week of July.
Henry Precisely for the second week of July.
All (*together*) From the tenth to the seventeenth.

A pause while the real horror of the situation sinks in

All (*together*) Chitto!
Mary Where is he?
Leslie He'll be back in a minute with the doctor.
Mary He'll need one.
Eve (*pleasantly*) Look, I know this isn't exactly what any of us planned, but it's a big house and we needn't get in each other's hair.
Leslie Yes! (*Chattily*) You can sometimes make really good friends on holiday. Last year in Scarborough, me and my mother . . .
Mary Mr Smith.
Leslie Oh call me Leslie, please.
Mary Mr Smith, it is one of my cardinal rules *never* to make friends on holiday.
Henry Rules are made to be broken aren't they?
Mary Shut up Henry! (*To Leslie*) When did you sign your timeshare agreement?
Eve Last Easter. I bought it with a legacy.
Mary How interesting. When was it you signed yours, Henry?
Henry Just before Christmas. Four months earlier! (*To Leslie and Eve*) So kindly vacate our premises as soon as possible.

Eve leans forward and whispers something in Mary's ear. It could be very rude. Mary draws in her breath with a hiss

Mary Throw them out, Henry.
Henry Just a sec, dear. As the little lady said it's a big house. We need hardly meet. And look at the size of that garden! It's large enough for the four of us to lie behind bushes and sunbathe in the altogether.
Mary Henry . . . !
Henry But not too close together.
Mary I said, "Throw them out".
Eve If he lays a finger on me I'll push his face in.
Henry May I strongly counsel you against that? I happen to be a lawyer. I suggest we wait until the Commander comes and we can sort the matter out legally and peacefully.

Leslie Good idea. Meanwhile, I'm starving. Do you think you could let us have some of our dinner?
Mary *Your* dinner?
Eve Yes, *our* dinner. We went and bought the bloody polo.
Mary Language!
Eve Oh, I'm sorry. Bloody chicken.
Mary There should be some bits and pieces left over from it. Come along, Henry.

Mary exits into the kitchen

Henry follows her, raising two finger to Leslie as he goes

Henry I'll save the wishbone for you.

Henry exits into the kitchen, not quite closing the door

Eve Chitto'll never sort this out, so what are we going to do about those two?
Leslie We should pack it in and leave. We're doomed.
Eve Why do you say that?
Leslie What if Syd rings again and that Charlesworth woman answers it?

Unseen by them, Henry's head appears in the kitchen doorway, then disappears, but the door remains ajar

He'll say "Is that Sister Esperanza? Can I speak to my wife, Eve?" The cat'll be out of the bag, and he'll hop over here and do me. I'll be six feet under, like Charley.

Henry enters from the kitchen

Henry Sorry to interrupt you lovebirds, but the situation has resolved itself.
Eve You're leaving.
Henry No, you are. You're not married, are you?
Leslie He's been listening!
Eve I've got news for you. What we're doing is not illegal, bat ears.
Henry I know what's legal or illegal. I'm a lawyer, remember.
Eve So what can you do about it? Nothing.
Henry Well, if Syd calls up, or if I call Syd ...
Eve You don't know his number.
Henry My dear girl, with my contacts in the police and the underworld, I could have his number and Syd out here in a matter of hours.
Leslie You wouldn't!
Henry Wouldn't I? You just try me!
Leslie All right, all right. We give up. You win.
Eve (*shocked*) Leslie!
Leslie It's no good. Let's just get out of here as soon as we can.
Henry Fine. No hurry. Any time in the next five minutes.

Henry exits into the kitchen

(*As he goes*) Case closed, darling.
Leslie Eve, I'm sorry ...
Eve Sorry! Have you no guts, no blood in your veins?

Leslie Yes, and frankly I want to keep it there.

Eve I can't believe this. You know, I really thought we had something going.

Leslie We did.

Eve Oh, forget it. I'll get the bags.

Eve exits DL

Henry and Mary enter from kitchen. She carries a dustpan and brush. He carries sandwiches wrapped in paper which he hands to Leslie

Henry Ah, Smith. Mary has made you up a few sandwiches for the journey.

Leslie (*sarcastically*) Thank you, Mary.

Mary Nice to have met you, Mr Smith. Well, as there's no Pedro and Maria, I'll give the bedroom a going over.

Henry, all smiles and good cheer, kisses her

Henry Before I do the same to you.

Mary likes this, smiles, then exits through archway DR

Henry is stopped from following her by the front doorbell ringing

(*To Leslie*) That'll be Chitto. Tell him the problem's solved; but have a word about a refund. You're due one.

Leslie With my luck and his brains he'll send the refund to you.

Henry chuckles and exits DR

Leslie goes to the front door and opens it

Are you pickled?

Celia Partridge appears outside and comes through the doorway. She is a county lady who is, at times, apt to mis-hear what is said, but carries this off with great aplomb. She carries a raffia beach bag and her neck is festooned with chains carrying an assortment of spectacles, perfume bottle, pen, fan, fob watch, etc

Celia No, Partridge.

Leslie Oh, pardon!

Celia Partridge. Celia Partridge. I'm looking for my son-in-law. He's staying here with an old pal.

Leslie I don't think so.

Celia Oh yes he is. Hold this, will you?

Celia hands Leslie the raffia bag. She starts to rummage through the bag which is full of assorted junk

It's in here somewhere. The address. (*She produces a box of chocolates*) Chocs. Have one. Liqueurs. Look out for the cherry stone.

Leslie hasn't a hand to spare so shakes his head. She puts the chocolates back, rummages ever deeper, briefly producing, among other things, a banana and a fly swat

I definitely jotted it down on a piece of paper. Ah, here we are! (*She produces a piece of paper and puts her glasses on*) Oh, no! That's a gas bill. Now why did I bring that to Portugal? (*She starts to put it back, then stops*) Oh yes! That's what I wrote it on! You see? L'Aranjina. This is the Villa L'Aranjina?

Leslie Yes . . . And what was the name again?

Celia Oh, dear! (*Loudly and distinctly*) Partridge. Celia Partridge.

Leslie No, *his* name. Your son-in-law.

Celia Charlesworth. Henry Charlesworth.

Leslie Oh, yes. He's just through there.

Henry enters through the archway DR. *At the sight of Celia he freezes*

Henry Mumpots!

Celia Henry!

Henry Mumpots!

Celia Surprise! Surprise! And do drop that stupid "Mumpots"! (*To Leslie*) My daughter detests him calling me that.

Leslie Oh, your daughter. She's in . . .

Henry (*quickly*) She's in London.

Leslie In London?

Henry ENGLAND!

Leslie England.

Henry (*loudly and desperately*) Old boy, this is my mother-in-law . . . Married to my father-in-law, mother of my wife, *Catherine.*

Leslie Catherine?

A smile crosses Leslie's face as the penny drops

Henry Catherine. And my wife, *who is back in London* . . .

Leslie England.

Henry England! Is her daughter.

Celia I trust that gives him some idea of who I am! (*She points to Leslie*) And you don't have to tell me who this is.

Leslie opens his mouth, but Henry moves close to him speaking fast

Henry I don't have to, but I am going to. This is my old school chum from Harrow . . .

Leslie Harrow?

Henry Harrow, Oxford and Sandhurst, who is staying here with me for a week in the best bedroom, with the run of the house, unlimited booze, a free car and all reasonable expenses. He and I have flown down for our usual week of golf; rather boring, but golf, pure and unadulterous— unadulterated.

Celia Of course I guessed! Who else but your golfing friend?

Henry Yes. This is Colonel Sir Piers Marchbanks.

Leslie Eh?

Celia Nice to meet you at last.

Henry Piers, say how do you do to Mumpots.

Henry pushes Leslie on the bottom to propel him forward

Leslie How do, Mumpots.

Leslie crosses to Celia and slaps her playfully on the bottom

Henry collapses behind the sofa

CURTAIN

ACT II

The same

The action is continuous

Celia (*looking all around*) Where's Henry gone? Where did he go?

Henry's head slowly appears from behind the sofa

Ah, there you are, Henry. What are you doing down there?
Henry Er—kneeling.
Celia Very flattering! Why?
Henry You've heard of Tennis Elbow?
Celia Yes.
Henry Well, I have Golfer's Knees.
Celia I never heard of that.
Henry Quite common in hot climates. Right, Piers? Piers!

Leslie clicks his heels and salutes

Leslie Oh, absotively bloominlutely.
Celia Does it happen when he's whacking his balls about?
Leslie Pardon?

Celia waves her arms in a golf swing

Celia On the links.
Leslie Oh, ya, ya. Absobloomintivelylutely.

*Henry's expression betrays the fact that he doesn't care for Leslie's perform-
ance as a "toff"*

Henry Yes, it often does.
Leslie Yes, often.

Henry has now risen

Celia (*to Leslie*) But if he's on his knees half the time, how does he play you?
Leslie Er—he uses very short sticks.
Celia Did you say "sticks"?

Henry lets out a dreadfully phoney hearty laugh

Henry Ha! Ha! That's the real golf aficionado talking, Mumpots.
Celia Is it?
Henry (*gabbling*) Yes. We sticklers call them "sticks" because we know we
  mean "clubs". It's only the amateur rabbit who calls sticks "clubs"

because, if he calls clubs "sticks" it sticks out a mile that he's new at the club ...
Celia I think you're burbling, Henry.
Henry Yes, I think I am. (*He pats his leg*) That's another of the symptoms.
Celia How very nasty! I see it makes you perspire, too.
Henry *Always*. Right, Piers?
Leslie Oh, ya. Absotively lutely bloomin!
Celia Most unfortunate. (*To Leslie*) Must spoil your fun. I gather you're a madly keen player.
Leslie Oh, ya, madly.
Celia Have you ever played in The Open?
Leslie Yes, when it isn't raining.
Henry (*quickly*) There he goes again! That old golfer's chestnut! He's too much. (*He kisses Celia heartily*) Mumpots, it's great to have you here.
Celia Is it? I'm rather puzzled by one thing, Henry.
Henry Oh, God ... Oh, really?
Celia You haven't asked what I'm doing here.
Henry I knew there was something. What the f ... What *are* you doing here?
Celia Driving down to see Sybil Delamere at Praia de Rocha. It's only a little detour, so I thought I'd drop in and surprise you.
Henry You did, didn't she, Piers?
Leslie Oh ya, abso ...
Henry Oh, shut up! And how long are you staying, Mumpots?
Celia Only a week.
Henry A week!

Henry collapses backwards; but Leslie, who is behind him, catches him and stands him up again

A week *here*?
Celia No! An hour at the most.
Henry But you said a week.
Celia I mean I'm staying a week with Sybil. Nice of you to ask me, but I have to get on.
Henry Wonderful! What a shame! You haven't time for a quick drink before you go?
Celia Yes, I think I have. Something soft and long and fruity.
Henry No sooner said.

Henry picks up a bowl of fruit and goes to the bar

Celia I understand you're a great sportsman, Sir Piers.
Leslie Am I?
Celia Apart from golf you have another string to your bow.
Leslie Archery.
Celia No.

Henry mimes a cricket stroke

Leslie Baseball?

Henry shakes his head, bowls a ball

Bowls?

Henry angrily raises his fist at Leslie

Boxing?

Celia You're a real all-rounder, aren't you?

Leslie Am I?

Henry Yes, but Mumpots was referring to cricket, weren't you, Mumpots?

Celia Yes, of course.

Leslie Oh, that old thing, old thing.

Celia Henry's always raving about some innings of yours against the RAF.

Leslie (*cautiously*) Oh, is he?

Henry One of the finest matches I've ever watched, but he hates talking about it.

Celia I'm sure he doesn't.

Leslie Yes.

Celia (*to Henry*) There you are! He says he wants to. (*To Leslie*) Where was it?

Leslie Where was it? It was—er . . .

Henry mines a couple of boobs

Leslie Breast.

Henry makes an angry gesture with a banana

Cockfosters.

Henry holds two halves of a lemon to his chest

Bristols. (*Henry holds up just one*) Bristol.

Celia You've played everywhere, haven't you.

Leslie Oh, all over.

Celia Not surprising with your family background.

Leslie My background?

Celia Yes, your maternal grandfather.

Leslie Oh, the mater's pater?

Celia He played for England, did he not?

Leslie Did he not!

Celia Now, what was his name?

Leslie We just called him Grandad.

Henry involuntarily squirts soda on the carpet

Henry Isn't he a hoot? Strachan, wasn't it? Charles Strachan. Yes, he got a cap didn't he, Piers?

Leslie (*gaining confidence again*) Oh ya, for being one of England's finest batsmen.

Celia (*frowning*) A bowler, surely?

Leslie No, I think he got the bowler when he retired.

Henry looks like throttling Leslie but is sidetracked as Celia laughs

Henry What's the matter, Mumpots?
Celia I've just seen the joke.
Henry About the bowler?
Celia No, about playing golf in the open when it isn't raining!
Henry You're going to love the next one. Here, get this down you. You'll feel a lot better.

Henry approaches Celia with a beer mug absolutely crammed with fruit and with an unpeeled banana sticking up provocatively. Celia and Leslie stare at it, quite stunned

Everything all right?
Celia I feel fine. It's you who seem to be on edge.
Henry No, I'm as cume as a carcumber ... Come as a cue ...

Henry's voice trails away as Eve enters DL, *carrying a suitcase. She is grim-faced and looks coldly at Leslie*

Eve I'm ready.
Henry (*hastily*) Piers, old man, it's your wife. It's Amanda.
Eve What?
Leslie Oh, Amanda, yes, so it is! It's the jolly old wifey. (*He kisses Eve and winks at her*) Pip pip, old fruity!
Eve What are you talking like that for?
Henry And you never looked more radiant, *Amanda.*
Eve Amanda?
Leslie Amanda.
Henry And how was your journey?
Eve Journey?
Henry From London.
Leslie (*To Celia*) England.
Henry She's just arrived. They always travel separately because of the children. Piers, old son, could you introduce Amanda to my mum-in-law. (*To Celia*) She's great fun. You'll love her.
Celia I'm sure I shall.
Leslie Amanda, this is—the mother-in-law of my old school chum from Wembley ...
Henry Harrow!
Leslie Harrow. She's the mother of his wife, *who is not here.*
Eve But I thought ...
Henry (*cutting in*) I know! You thought she might be coming out, too, but she isn't. She's back in England, leaving me on my ownsome with you, Amanda and Piers.
Eve (*getting there*) Oh, I see. I see!
Celia So you are Lady Marchbanks?
Eve (*in a posh voice*) Lady Marchbanks!
Celia I just don't believe it.
Henry Please! You must!
Celia I imagined you to be much older.
Leslie Oh, she is!

Henry But you'd never know it. Doesn't she look terrific?

Celia Lovely, but you always said that wives were strictly banned from these golfing holidays.

Henry True, Mumpots, but she's been desperately ill. That's why she looks so awful!

Celia (*bemused*) Didn't you just say she looked terrific?

Henry (*considering*) But it was touch and go and she just had to get away to the sun.

Celia I'm so sorry to hear you've been unwell.

Eve Sick as a parrot.

Celia Oh, dear! What did you have!

Eve (*looking for help*) What did the quack say it was?

Leslie ⎱ (*together*) ⎰ Whooping cough.
Henry ⎰   ⎱ Chicken pox.

Leslie Whooping Chicken.

Henry Cough Pox.

Celia (*laughing*) I think *I* must have a touch of the sun. For a moment I thought you said cough pox!

All laugh heartily at this. Offstage DR *comes a crash and a cry from Mary*

Henry (*panicking*) Oh, God! Excuse me. Have to tie something up in the bedroom.

Leslie While you're at it I should gag it as well.

Henry moves R *but stops as—*

Mary enters from door DR. *She is carrying the dustpan and has tied a scarf round her head to keep her hair in place*

Mary I . . .

Henry (*shouting desperately*) Not now, *Maria!* (*He wags a finger in her face*) Voo no entrada in la sitting-room sans knockos. Moltos rudos. Comprende, *Maria*?

Mary Wha . . .

Henry *Silenzio!* Unos verbos mas und voo riskos the sackos. Comprende *Maria*? (*He turns apologetically to Celia*) Sorry about this, Mumpots; just explaining. These servants have to understand who's the boss.

Celia If I heard you correctly she'll never understand that gibberish.

Henry She'd better! She'll pull her socks up once she knows you're my *mother-in-law.*

Mary is so shocked by this revelation that she shoots dust from the pan all over everyone. Celia dusts herself down then approaches Mary

Celia (*fluently*) Boa tarde. Eu chamone Senhora Patridge—em Portuguese "Perdiz". Ha! Ha! Eu sou sogre deste senhor. Nao se preoccupe em razer a cama, porque eu nao vou ficar de noite.

Mary looks totally blank

Henry (*uneasily*) What language was that, Mumpots?

Celia Portuguese, of course.

Henry I guessed as much; but you're wasting your time. She doesn't speak a word of Portuguese; but you are quite amazing! Isn't she amazing?

Leslie Amazing!

Eve Amazing!

Henry What languages *don't* you speak, Mumpots?

Celia Now, that's a poser! I think I get by in all of them.

Leslie Amazing!

Eve Amazing!

Celia No, I lie.

Henry Oh, good!

Celia I don't speak a word of Hungarian.

Henry Isn't that typical? Typical! What awful luck!

Leslie Oh! Awful!

Eve Awful!

Henry You might have brought a smile to that sullen, Slavic face.

Celia Why?

Henry Maria Gabor is from Budapest and doesn't speak a word of any other language but her own.

Celia So she's Hungarian? How does she come to be in Portugal?

Leslie Walked, by the look of her.

Henry Piers! (*Then to Mary*) Allez dans la cuccina. (*To Leslie*) I'm sorry you should have to witness this—Sir Piers and Lady Marchbanks.

Celia What on earth are you talking like that for, Henry?

Henry Like what for?

Celia Like some stammering robot, explaining names and relationships as if nobody has ever heard them before.

Henry (*indicating Mary*) She hadn't.

Celia But you said she didn't understand a word.

Henry You never know, something might sink in.

Eve I doubt it. She's as thick as two planks, that one, eh, sweetie?

Leslie Yes, my angel—a real pain in the crutchos.

Celia Do be careful. You shouldn't talk like that, even though she does look rather disagreeable.

Leslie She's got very shifty eyes.

Eve Specially the right one.

Mary stamps on Henry's foot and flounces out into kitchen

Henry limps after her

Celia The old golfer's knee playing up again?

Henry Yes. Excuse me, I'm just going to read her the riot act.

Celia I hope you can read it in Hungarian.

Eve You've got a point there.

Celia (*to Henry*) And perhaps you'd ask her to make me a pot of tea.

Henry I'll do my best. (*As he exits*) Maria, eine tiapot for meine Mumpot.

Henry exits into kitchen

Celia If I'm not mistaken, my dear, wasn't your father a Hogg?

Eve Occasionally, when he'd had a skinful.
Celia Skinful?
Leslie (*hastily*) That was a joke.
Celia Of course, your mother and I went to Roedean together.
Eve Oh? I hope the weather kept fine.
Celia (*apparently ignoring this*) Yes, we were at school together, Roedean.
Leslie Whereabouts in Roedean?

Celia gives Leslie a little slap on the arm with her fan

Celia Most amusing, but you don't fool me! I know exactly what you two are up to.

Leslie and Eve look alarmed

Leslie Oh.
Celia Yes! You're pulling my leg. But I don't mind. I hate the young treating me with too much respect; makes me feel my age. (*She fans herself*) I'm feeling the heat. If there's a pool, I might have a quick dip.
Eve There is one, just below the "terrarce".
Celia Good. I brought a costume on the offchance. (*She moves to the window*) Oh, what a gorgeous rose arbour! (*She takes a skimpy costume from her bag*) Ah, there it is!

Celia exits via the balcony

Eve moves closer to Leslie

Eve Do I take it, Sir Galahad has decided to stay and fight?
Leslie You bet. We've got Mister Henry Charlesworth by the short and curlies—and he knows it.
Eve So forget Mister Nice Guy and put the screws on like they did.

There is the sound of a plate smashing, and angry voices from the kitchen

He's got troubles in there, too!
Henry (*off*) Aaaagh!

Henry enters from the kitchen, bent a little forward as the result of a blow

Henry Sorry about that. Just a little fracas in the kitchen.
Eve Very volatile, these Hungarians.
Leslie Where did she get you—in the goulash?
Henry (*acidly*) Very funny.

Eve suddenly laughs

And what are you laughing at?
Eve I've only just got it—in the goulash!

Celia enters through the french windows, chuckling to herself

Celia I've only just got it.
Henry Join the club!
Celia Most amusing.
Henry Glad you think so.

Celia (*to Leslie*) Your Grandad's cap was a bowler! No wonder Henry finds you so witty.
Leslie Have you heard the one about the fracas in the goulash . . . ?
Henry NO! Old boy, isn't it time for your little siesta?
Leslie I'm quite happy sitting here chatting to Mumpots.
Eve I'd rather have a little siesta. Come on.

Eve exits DL *with suitcase*

Leslie walks to door UL *then turns*

Leslie Oh, by the way, Henry.
Henry What?
Leslie I just remembered. You never paid me for beating you at golf this morning.
Henry Didn't I?
Leslie No, you didn't. So you owe me a hundred and fifty on the match.
Henry Hundred and fifty! As much as that?
Leslie At least. And I will get it by tonight, won't I?
Henry (*through clenched teeth*) You'll get it, I promise you. You'll get it.

Leslie exits DL

Celia (*loudly*) *Henry!*
Henry Yes, Mumpots.
Celia I'm deeply shocked!
Henry What about?
Celia I've just realized what you're doing here. It's disgusting. You just gave the game away, didn't you?

Henry's legs give way again

Henry How . . . I don't know what you're talking about!
Celia Yes, you do. Once you men get involved, there's no controlling it.
Henry Mumpots. It was just a moment of folly.
Celia Rubbish! You're banging away every day.
Henry Mumpots!
Celia Probably twice a day.
Henry Really!
Celia Gambling as high as that on a game of golf! It's beyond a joke.
Henry Oh! Gangling—bangling—gamble banging—gambling. You mean *gambling*?
Celia Yes. A hundred and fifty pounds on one stupid game!
Henry *Escudos*, Mumpots! Escudos! Less than a quid! Chicken feed.
Celia Escudos!
Henry Yes! I'm a reformed character when it comes to gambling. Ask anyone. Ask Catherine.
Celia Oh! Then I take it all back. And you must do something about those legs of yours. No wonder you're losing the matches.
Henry I will. Promise. (*Vastly relieved*) Whew!

There is the sound of a car crash outside

Chitto (*off*) Mayday! Mayday!
Celia That sounds like an accident.
Henry It is. I'm going to try and keep it out of here.

Henry hurries to the front door, opens it

 Chitto more or less falls into his arms. His hat is pulled over his eyes

Chitto No bones broken, but I think I've gone blind.

Henry rather roughly pulls Chitto's hat up

 Oh, that's better.

Henry and Chitto come into the room

Henry What happened?
Chitto It was that wall. Stupid great thing, it never saw me.
Celia Henry, who is this?
Henry Commander Chittenden of Share-a-Lux. (*In an undertone*) Lush.

Henry goes to the trolley to pour a glass of water. Chitto turns and looks at Celia

Chitto Oh, hello! You're looking as pretty as ever, my dear.
Celia (*blankly*) As ever?
Chitto (*confidentially*) You'll be pleased to know, I've reported the matter of the poisoned bird to the police, Mrs Charlesworth.
Celia Partridge, actually.
Chitto Really? Now, why did I think it was chicken?
Celia I beg your pardon?
Chitto Still, a poisoned partridge is equally lethal.

Henry gestures to Celia to take no notice

Celia Poisoned? I don't understand.

Henry brings Chitto a drink

Henry Don't even try, Mumpots.
Celia (*in an undertone*) Obviously delirious.
Henry Obviously. You drink this down by the pool and drop in any time.
Chitto And all the evidence points to Pedro and Maria administering a poisoned partridge to Colonel Wagstaff.
Celia Colonel who?
Henry Wagstaff.
Celia Who is he?
Henry It doesn't matter.
Celia Surely it must matter to Colonel Wagstaff?
Henry Not any more. He's dead.
Celia Dead?
Chitto As a dodo.
Celia Dear! Dear!
Chitto Done to death by his domestics.

Celia Good gracious! (*She looks towards the kitchen*) And are you saying that one of them is that sour-faced Hungarian ...?

Chitto (*irritably*) No! I'm talking about Pedro and Maria the poisonous Portuguese. (*Late reaction*) Hungarian? (*To Henry, indicating Celia*) Who is this lady?

Henry Mother-in-law.

Chitto Colonel Wagstaff's mother-in-law?

Celia No!

Chitto I was going to say. For a start, he wasn't married. Confirmed bachelor. (*He winks at Celia*) Know what I mean?

Celia No, I don't. I don't understand a word you're saying.

Chitto I'm saying the Colonel was killed in cold blood by Pedro and Maria.

There is a crash offstage DL

By God, they're at it again!

Another crash offstage and a scream from Eve

Leslie enters DL *carrying a piece of the fourposter*

Leslie You know that fourposter? Well it's a threeposter now.

Chitto Now look here Pedro ...

Henry (*loudly*) Wrong!

Chitto Really? (*He walks over to peer closely at Leslie. He recognizes him*) Oh, a million apologies! It's Mr Smith, isn't it?

Henry Wrong!

Chitto Wrong?

Chitto consults his clipboard. Leslie moves away as:

Eve enters DL *and takes his place*

Chitto looks up and now sees Eve

Correction—*Mrs* Smith.

Henry Wrong!

Chitto Wrong?

Eve Wrong!

Chitto No! No! This is impossible. It's down here— Eve and Leslie Smith.

Henry Let's have a recap on names.

Chitto I'm all for that.

Henry This is my mother-in-law, Mrs Partridge, and this is Amanda, Lady Marchbanks and Colonel Sir Piers Marchbanks.

Chitto I give up! There's no mention of Marchbanks here or a Mrs Plover.

Celia Partridge.

Chitto Or a blasted Partridge.

Eve lets out a strangled laugh. Henry glares at her

Mary, carrying a pot of tea on a tray, enters from the kitchen

Mary (*rudely*) Oi!

Celia Oi?

Henry Oi veh Maria!
Celia What does that mean?
Henry I'm not sure.
Leslie I expect it's Hungarian for "Thank you, Maria".
Mary Char.
Eve And that'll be Hungarian for tea.

Mary puts the tray down. Her journey takes her close to Chitto, who points a triumphant finger at her

Chitto Aha! Now, I don't want to appear over-confident, but I am right, am I not, Mr Charlesworth, in saying that this is your wife, Mrs Charlesworth?
Henry Wrong!
Leslie Wrong!
Eve Wrong!
Celia Wrong!
Chitto Wrong? I'm not going to like the answer, but who is this lady, then?
Henry This is Maria, the maid.
Chitto Ah! (*Severely to Mary*) Now listen to me. I have reported you to the police and as soon as he has a moment he'll be up with the black Maria Maria, Maria Maria, Maria Maria.
Celia Am I going mad, or is he now singing *West Side Story*?
Henry Yes.
Celia In that case I'm going to have that dip.
Chitto What a good idea! Scotch, vodka . . . ?
Celia *Dip*, not nip and it might do *you* good, too, Commander.
Chitto No, thanks. Never touch water.
Eve We can vouch for that, can't we, Sir Piers?
Leslie Oh, absobloomin . . .

Henry cuffs Leslie

Ow!
Chitto But I'll join you. The fresh air might clear my head.

Chitto and Celia move to the french windows

Now, you did say your name was Penguin?

Chitto and Celia exit R *on balcony*

Mary (*loudly*) Now listen, Henry . . .
Henry (*agonised*) Ssssh! Careful.
Mary No, I don't want to be careful. Just tell your mother-in-law the truth.
Henry The truth?
Mary That you want to divorce Catherine and marry me.
Henry Ye—es but, please, not in front of them.
Leslie Don't worry about us.
Eve No. Let your hair down.
Mary So when she comes back simply present her with the facts.

Leslie That sounds reasonable, and we can all stop this stupid pretending . . .

Henry (*turning on Leslie*) Will you shut up! When I want your help I'll ask for it.

Eve You did ask for it.

Mary Well, we don't need it any more.

Leslie Please yourself.

Mary Think calmly, Henry. I know you're overwrought . . .

Henry I'm not overwrought, I'm overdrawn.

Mary You can't be. You're a highly successful barrister.

Henry All legal aid cases. I earn a pittance.

Mary But you have pots of money . . .

Henry It's all Catherine's. Catherine's money subsidises me.

Eve (*giggling*) He's a kept man.

Henry (*without thinking*) Objection!

Mary Over-ruled. You never told me this. You've been leading me on all this time, dangling your prospects in front of me.

Leslie Naughty, Henry! You can get six months for that.

Henry Belt up!

Leslie I'm sorry, your Honour. Would you care for a glass of the plonko bianco, Amanda?

Eve Spiffing idea, Sir Piers.

Henry (*to Mary*) I'm taking silk next year. Can't you wait for that?

Mary In the meantime I have to grovel around pretending to be a skivvy.

Henry Only for an hour until Mumpots leaves.

Mary It's ridiculous. I'd have been far more suitable as Lady Marchbanks. You only have to listen to this girl.

Eve (*hotly*) I've been a damn sight better in my part than what you have, Maria.

Mary There she goes again!

Leslie All right, if you don't like the way we're doing it, we'll pack it in and we'll tell Mumpots the truth.

Henry Wait, Leslie, see me safely through this and the villa's yours for the week.

Leslie Now you're talking!

Eve I wouldn't believe a word that liar says.

Henry How dare you! I only lie to one person in this world and that is my wife.

Chitto and Celia enter through the French window

Celia Henry . . . ?

Henry I deny it!

Henry drops to his knees, swivels round and looks at Celia

Celia What's going on?

Henry Nothing!

Celia Is it your golfer's knees again?

Leslie No he's got cold feet now.

Henry (*getting up*) I thought you were having a swim.

Celia I decided against it.

Henry Why?

Chitto She spotted a fellow she didn't like lurking in the pool.

Celia No, I didn't! All I said was: "Oh, dear, there's algae".

Chitto How she recognized him I'll never fathom. Water's like pea soup. (*To Mary*) Pedro should be dealing with that. Have a word with him, Maria.

Mary (*sullenly*) Si, Senhor.

Leslie And let's have a little smile while you're on the job.

Mary Si, Senhor.

Eve And you may leave the Tia Maria.

Mary Si senhora. Obrigado. Bom dia with nobs on.

Mary gives a snarl-like smile and exits into kitchen

Celia I know I get things muddled, but I thought you said Maria didn't speak a word of English or Portuguese?

Henry I gave her a crash course.

There is heard a crash from the kitchen

Eve And she's started another one.

Henry (*hastily*) Piers, old chap, why don't you take that b . . . beautiful wife of yours for a stroll in the garden?

Leslie Right. (*To Eve*) Amanda, my dear, let's try our luck in the arbour.

Eve The 'arbour? Lovely! We can see all the little fishing boats.

Leslie and Eve exit via the balcony

Celia I feel a bit peckish. Do you think Maria could knock me up a sandwich?

Henry I wouldn't advise it, Mumpots. She's very heavy on the garlic.

Celia I like garlic.

Henry But you might be breathalysed.

Celia I'm not going until I've had something to eat.

Henry Well, I'll see what I can do about it. (*He opens the kitchen door*) Memsahib Mumpots wantee chop suey chop-chop. How do you feel about it?

A plate is heard to shatter. Henry ducks

Henry exits into the kitchen, closing the door

Celia Between you and me, Commander, I don't think my son-in-law and that maid are going to hit it off. Tell me, is her husband Hungarian, too?

Chitto Why on earth should he be Hungarian?

Celia Well, she is.

Chitto What!

Celia She comes from Budapest, but I doubt if she's related to Zsa Zsa Gabor.

Chitto Mrs Puffin, I've noticed, since you arrived, that you haven't made a lot of sense. Be careful. You could be heading for the old Portuguese problem.

Celia What are you talking about?

Chitto Lifting the old elbow too high and too often.

Celia Are you suggesting I drink too much?

Chitto Well, you wouldn't be the first.

Celia (*outraged*) I haven't had a drink since I arrived!

Chitto Good Lord! We'll soon make up for that. What's your poison?

Celia A small sherry, thank you.

Chitto picks up a sherry glass

Chitto No problem.

Celia Make it a medium, if possible.

Chitto That's what I like to hear!

Chitto puts down the sherry glass and picks up a half pint beer glass which he fills with sherry

Girl after my own heart.

Chitto hands her the tumbler, which she looks at with dismay

Celia Steady the buffs! I want to keep my wits about me.

Chitto (*drinking*) Good health. Ah, that's better. First of the day.

Celia Really?

Chitto Well, not counting those for medicinal purposes.

Celia May I confide in you, Commander?

Chitto If you must, but try to make it simple. One can only absorb so much in one day.

Celia (*looking at his glass*) It seems to me that you absorb quite a lot.

Chitto You have to in this job. Always problems. So what can I do for you?

Celia To be very frank, I've been a little suspicious about my son-in-law's golfing holidays: you know, wondering if he wasn't playing around with another woman.

Chitto Well, there are plenty of good women golfers about.

Celia No, I didn't mean that.

Chitto Here we go again! What did you mean?

Celia I meant playing around with another woman.

Chitto So you said. One round or several?

Celia No! (*She lowers her voice*) Having an *affaire* with another woman.

Chitto On the golf course?

Celia Anywhere.

Chitto Well, so long as they keep it in the rough.

Celia Commander, try to get your mind off golf.

Chitto That's easily done. Can't stand the game. Boring.

Celia Exactly what Henry used to say; but now, recently, he shoots off twice a year, ostensibly to play golf with his friend, Piers Marchbanks.

Chitto Getting a bit old for squash, perhaps!

Celia But not too old for the roving eye. Now, my daughter, Catherine, is somewhat naive in these matters and believes in him implicitly. I may be an old cynic, but I seized on this opportunity of popping in unexpectedly and possibly catching him out.

Chitto But you caught him in, so no worry there.

Celia On the surface everything seems to be as it should be; and I hope you'll confirm that it is?

Chitto Yes, I think so, apart from typical Portuguese problems with the curtains and staff.

Celia What problems?

Chitto They keep falling down.

Celia The staff?

Chitto No, the curtains.

Celia Do you think we might return to the point?

Chitto Well, we can but try. What was it?

Celia Um—yes, what was it? Now you've put it right out of my mind.

Chitto Something to do with your drink problem?

Celia (*angrily*) I do not have a drink problem Colonel Wagstaff.

Chitto Wagstaff? I could have sworn my name was Chittenden ...

Celia I meant Chittenden.

Chitto Good! Well done! Now, where were we?

Celia I know. My son-in-law.

Chitto And his name is ... ?

Celia Henry Charlesworth.

Chitto Right again. Spot on.

Celia So I take it that I have nothing to worry about concerning his behaviour here?

Chitto Absolutely.

Celia Splendid! Then I can carry on with an easy mind. (*She lowers her voice*) Of course, I don't have to tell you that this conversation never took place.

Chitto (*amazed*) Didn't it?

Celia No.

Chitto Good Lord! Then what were we talking about?

Celia I want you to forget it.

Chitto I have. That's why I'm asking you. Um—can I offer you a drink?

Celia No! I can't even finish this one. It's enormous.

Chitto Yes, by Jove. It is rather. Did I warn you about the old Portuguese problem?

Celia Yes.

Chitto Doesn't seem to have sunk in. That's a very hefty drink, Madam.

Celia Which *you* poured me.

Chitto You sure?

Celia Positive. Tell me Commander, have you ever suffered from amnesia?

Chitto Er—I forget.

Celia puts down her glass and moves to the French windows

Celia Well, do try to remember what I said about our conversation.

Chitto Certainly. What was it?

Celia Forget it. Just forget it.

Celia exits R *onto the balcony*

Henry enters from the kitchen

Henry Mumpots, the sandwiches are . . .

Chitto I'm a bit worried about your Mrs Parrot.

Henry Partridge. I'm worried, but why are you?

Chitto For a start, see the size of that drink she had? (*He lifts glass*) That isn't ginger ale, you know.

Henry Commander, I want to confide in you.

Chitto Oh, dear!

Henry I want to talk to you about my wife.

Chitto So do I, because your Mrs Pigeon has certainly put the cat among the partridges.

Henry Listen, please. The lady I introduced as my wife isn't actually my wife.

Chitto We're off again!

Henry She's my girl friend and it won't have escaped your notice that she's also Maria, the maid.

Chitto (*amazed*) You mean you walked in, took one look at the maid and it was love at first sight?

Henry No! We've been going steady for two years.

Chitto Two years? How does old Pedro feel about that?

Henry There isn't a Pedro.

Chitto Oh, yes there is.

Henry All right, but not the one you think is Pedro.

Chitto (*losing the thread*) You mean he's not married to Maria?

Henry Yes, of course he is, but to the *other* Maria.

Chitto What other Maria?

Henry The *real* Maria. But, anyway, forget Pedro because he doesn't come into it.

Chitto shakes his head and downs his drink

Let's stick with Maria who, of course, isn't Maria but was introduced to you as Mrs Charlesworth, which, of course, she isn't either. Her name is Mary. And the other couple, known as Colonel Sir Piers and Lady Marchbanks are, in fact, Leslie and Eve Smith. Marchbanks—that is, Smith—and I are supposed to be having a golfing holiday here but actually, of course, Marchbanks isn't here at all. He's in the Algarve with *his* bird. Still, we've got to continue the deception until there's no danger of Mrs Partridge acting as stool pigeon.

Beaten at last Chitto throws the clipboard over his shoulder

Chitto Abandon ship!

Henry Do you want me to start again?

Chitto NO!!

There is another crash from kitchen followed by an angry cry from Mary

Henry (*agitated*) Excuse me. This could be more trouble. By the way, Commander—I need hardly tell you this conversation never took place.

Henry exits into the kitchen, closing the door

Chitto, pole-axed, takes out his tape recorder

Chitto (*to recorder*) Miss Mogardo, I may sleep in tomorrow stop; so if you don't get this message you'll know why stop.

Front doorbell rings

Come in stop. (*Realizing*) Oh, excuse me. There's someone at the door stop. (*Moving towards door*) Not the door stop just the door—stop. Oh, do shut up! Come in.

Chitto opens the front door and stands back, partially obscuring himself from view

A genial gentleman in blazer, shirt, Harrovian tie and sunglasses bursts in. He will be known as Perky. He walks right past Chitto

Perky A thousand apologies. I know I'm the last person you wanted to see but the fact is there's been a catastrophic cock-up.
Chitto What?

Perky turns and removes his glasses

Perky Oh, I'm awfully sorry. I thought you'd be Pinky.
Chitto (*touching his own cheek*) I quite often am; but I tell the doctor not to worry. It's only blood pressure.
Perky (*laughs*) No, I mean I thought you were Pinky Charlesworth.
Chitto Pinky?
Perky He's Pinky and I'm Perky. Sounds silly I know. Dates from our schooldays at Harrow—always first to have our heads in the trough!
Chitto Pinky and Perky? Sounds vaguely familiar.
Perky If this is the right place he's got a time-share in this villa. (*He indicates height*) He's about so high and could be wearing a tie like mine—Harrow—without the egg on it.
Chitto Ah! Harrow! Got it! (*Wagging a finger*) Colonel Sir Piers Marchbanks, right?
Perky (*astonished*) Yes. Amazing! How could you possibly know?
Chitto Well, it's an unusual name and, for once, it sort of stuck.
Perky Then you're obviously in dear old Pinky's confidence about the little arrangement that he and I have for a week of so-called golf.
Chitto We're off again—golf.
Perky Golf. He with his girl friend, Mary.
Chitto Mary?
Perky Mary, and me with my little bird in the Algarve.
Chitto Algarve?
Perky Unfortunately mine threw a tantrum last night.
Chitto A tantrum?

Perky And a few other things and she's pushed off.
Chitto Off?
Perky I can't go back to my wife in England because that would land poor old Pinky in it with his; so I decided to pop in here for a council of war with dear old Pinky and dear old Mary. (*He sees Chitto looking blank*) Oh dear! I don't think you told me your name?
Chitto What? No, it's—er—just give me a second ... on the tip of my tongue—er—(*He wags a finger*) Give us a clue.
Perky Finger? No—thumb.

Chitto scratches an ear

Sounds like thumb? Bum? No ...
Chitto (*into recorder*) Miss Mogardo ...
Perky Mogardo? My God, I'd never have got it.
Chitto It's Chittenden here. Ah! Chittenden. (*To Perky*) Commander Chittenden. Hang on to that.
Perky Right.
Chitto Good. (*To recorder*) Sorry to trouble you.
Perky Not at all.
Chitto Now, apart from being Perky, what's your proper name?
Perky You know it. You just told me.
Chitto Did I? I don't remember. Could you just run through it again?
Perky In full? Well, I'm still Colonel Sir Piers Marchbanks.
Chitto (*pole-axed yet again*) That's impossible!
Perky Impossible? Why?
Chitto You're shorter.
Perky (*shouting*) I'm Marchbanks!
Chitto (*shaking his head*) Must be two other people.

Celia enters through the French windows

Celia Oh, hello.

Perky gives her a polite bow

Celia (*to Perky*) Excuse me a second. (*To Chitto*) I've just tripped over Lady Marchbanks ...
Perky (*reacts wildly*) Lady Ma ... Ma ... Ma ...!
Celia She was in the garden.
Perky In the ga ... ga ... ga ...?
Celia Lying in the arbour.
Perky In the arb ... arb ... bah?
Celia (*looking at him, puzzled*) I don't think we've met, have we?

Perky dumbly shakes his head

Henry enters from the kitchen

Henry Who's for pickles and ... ? (*He sees Perky and his knees go*) ... Perky!!!

Celia Oh, you two know each other! (*To Perky*) We haven't been introduced. I'm Celia Partridge. (*She holds out her hand*) And you are?

Henry (*sudden loud shout*) PEDRO!! This is Pedro.

Chitto Now I do give up.

Celia But I thought you said "Perky".

Henry Did I?

Celia Yes, you did.

Henry Yes, I did. That's his surname. He's Pedro Perky. He's Maria's husband and he's just arrived and he's the new manservant.

Celia Oh, Perki? With an "i", of course. Another Hungarian.

Perky A wha . . . ?

Henry Silensky Pedro! (*To the others*) Yes, this is Maria's husband, Pedro, who has finally arrived—and not a moment too soon. Probably with some feeble excuse like missing the bus.

Perky Ah, missy busky, busky . . .

Henry (*loudly*) Now listen to me very carefully. This lady is my mother-in-law, wife of my father-in-law, and mother of my wife, Catherine.

Celia (*confidentially to Henry*) Henry, is Pedro deaf?

Henry No just dumb.

Celia Then why are you shouting?

Henry Because it might sink in that Colonel Sir Piers Marchbanks, whom he has never met, *is already here.*

Perky gets the picture

Leslie and Eve enter through windows, chatting

Henry And lo and behold—here he is! Colonel Sir Piers Marchbanks. (*To Leslie*) And you'll be surprised when you find out who this is, old boy.

Leslie Will I?

Henry Yes, this is Pedro. (*Doing a golf stroke behind Celia's back*)

Leslie Pedro? Oh! Got it! (*In an undertone*) On his days off Pedro plays a little unadulterous golf?

Henry Absobloominlutely! (*To Perky*) Comprendo Pedro?

Perky Poco by poco.

Henry Goodo! And this is Amanda, Lady Marchbanks.

Perky (*vastly relieved*) Ah. That's Lady Ma-Ma-Ma from the arb-arb-bah!

Henry Ya! Ya! Ya!

Perky Thank Ga-ga-ga!

Chitto Excuse me, Madam, but who precisely did that fellow say he was?

Celia He—Pedro.

Chitto This could drive a lesser man to drink.

Chitto reels away, grabs a bottle of gin as he passes the bar and heads towards the french windows, eventually noticing the bottle in his hand

By God! It has.

Chitto exits via the balcony

Celia, a bit concerned, moves R to monitor Chitto's progress

Eve (*giggling at Perky*) I'll bet he never expected to walk in here and find Sir Piers and Lady Marchbanks!

Perky Absolutely notsky.

Henry And Pedro, your wife is in the kitchen—Maria. (*To Perky*) Portuguese for *Mary*.

Celia (*suddenly moving back*) But she's Hungarian!

Henry (*irritably startled*) He knows that. Don't muddle him.

Mary now enters from kitchen with a plate of rather thick sandwiches. She does not notice Perky as she heads towards Celia

Mary Sandwiches.

Perky Ciaou, Maria!

Mary turns and sees him

Mary Perky!

Mary is so startled that she shoots the sandwiches into the air and thence onto the floor

Henry (*hastily*) Yes, Maria! Your husband, Pedro Perki, has just arrived.

Perky Maria mia!

Perky enfolds Mary in a long embrace and pats her bottom. Henry angrily pushes his hand away

Celia They seem excessively overjoyed.

Henry Oh, they are. They're Latins!

Celia (*sharply*) Balkans!

Henry (*huffily*) All right, don't believe me.

Celia Amazing! I thought he only missed his bus.

Henry True, but that was a year ago in Budapest.

Celia Oh! What has he been doing in the meantime?

Henry Waiting for another one to come along. He's been stuck in the Urals. It's a shocking service.

Eve Like in here. Isn't anyone going to pick up those sandwiches?

Henry (*snapping his fingers*) Pedro! Maria! Sanvitchsky!

Perky and Mary gather up the fallen sandwiches and start putting them together again

Celia I do think the Commander should have organised a Portuguese couple for you.

Leslie Here! Here!

Celia I mean, how on earth are you going to communicate? One can't even tell her to make some more.

Perky (*launching into "Hungarian"*) Nishny noshny vinkov, Maria. Baka topola subotica budapesty sandwishsky. Ging gang gooly gooly goulash baka baker street, bakerloo, bake-a-cake.

Pedro escorts Maria into the kitchen

Celia What an impossible language! I'm glad I don't speak it.

Henry So am I.

Celia puts on her glasses and consults the fob watch on one of the chains

Celia Good gracious! Look at the time. I must be off.
Henry (*joyfully*) You're leaving?
Celia Yes. I have a long drive ahead of me.
Henry Oh, what a pity!
Eve Oh, stay a bit longer, do.
Leslie You can't go now, Mumpots.
Henry Yes, she can and she's not your Mumpots, she's my Mumpots. (*He pushes Celia towards front door*) It's been lovely to see you.
Celia And you.
Henry (*kissing her*) If you talk to Catherine before I do, give her a good report and tell her I'm missing her dreadfully.
Celia I will. Goodbye everyone. (*To Eve*) Sorry I kicked you in the arbour.
Eve No 'arm done.
Leslie Ta, ta, Mumpots!
Celia I'll just say goodbye to the Commander on my way to the car. (*She walks onto the balcony and looks over*) There he is, standing by the pool. (*She gives a start, reacts*) Commander! Stop that at once! You mustn't do that in the pool. (*To the others*) He's thrown his empty bottle in the water. Goodbye!

Celia exits R onto the balcony

There is a short pause for safety's sake, then Henry jumps for joy

Henry I did it! I did it!
Leslie What do you mean, "I did it"! *We* did it!
Henry Yes, and I can't thank you enough. This has been the worst hour of my life. (*He moves to Eve*) You're an angel. (*He kisses Eve, then approaches Leslie with open arms*) ... and Leslie ...
Leslie (*retreating*) Watch it!

The telephone rings. Henry picks it up

Henry Hullo? ... (*He checks the number on the phone*) Yes, this oh-oh-seven. ... Is this the whattery; ... No, it's nottery. (*He slams down the phone*) Some idiot thinks we're a nunnery.
Eve Hey! You shouldn't have done that. That's my husband and the nunnery is our alibi!

The telephone rings again. Leslie looks highly nervous

That'll be Syd again. (*To Henry*) Do you think you could ...
Henry No, I couldn't. It's your problem. You solve it.
Eve Oh, please!
Henry (*pompously*) I'm sorry, but, as a lawyer and a future QC, I cannot possibly condone adultery.
Eve Oh, thanks! I'll remember that.

Henry exits into the kitchen

Eve makes a rude gesture behind his back. She picks up telephone

Hello? . . . Oh, hello, Syd! Funny, I was thinking about you. Lucky you caught me. We've just come out of Vespers.

Leslie resumes his chanting and his bell ringing

Leslie (*chanting*) Te deum laudamus ars gratia artis sic transit Gloria sunday ad hoc ad nauseam.
Eve (*irritably*) Oh, shut up—Sister. (*Into the phone*) No, Syd, the phone hasn't rung here. You must have had a crossed line . . . There's no need to shout. It's not my fault . . . And watch your language . . . (*She cups the phone, turns to Leslie*) Do you know what he's just called me?
Leslie I don't care any more.
Eve (*hurt*) What?

Leslie grabs the receiver from Eve

Leslie Give me that! (*Into the phone*) Syd, it's me Leslie. No, it's not another crossed line. I happen to be here in Portugal.
Eve Are you mad?
Leslie Probably, but who cares? (*Into the phone*) No, Syd, I never was in Wales. I'm here at the nunnery and you'll never guess what I'm planning to do with Sister Eve . . . Well, that's not quite the word I'd have used, but it more or less sums it up. . . . And don't waste your money flying out here to duff me up, because we'll have moved on. Adios amigo, as we say in these parts . . . And the same to you, Syd, in your parts. (*He hangs up*)
Eve Do you realize what you've done?
Leslie Yes.
Eve Darling!

Eve goes to embrace Leslie but he suddenly sinks to his knees with the aftershock, leaving her to embrace air

Henry, Perky and Mary enter from the kitchen. Henry carries a tray of glasses full of champagne

Henry (*seeing the tableau*) Are we interrupting?
Eve No. Leslie's done something really mind-blowing.
Henry Oh? And has he finished?
Leslie (*rising*) I just told Syd where he gets off.
Perky Should I be told who Syd is?
Mary |
Henry } (*together*) NO!

Leslie Come on, Eve, let's re-christen that three-poster.
Eve (*impressed*) Leslie, there's more to you than I thought.
Leslie Well, hopefully there might be now. You haven't seen the half of it.

Eve and Leslie exit DL

Henry Oh, my little darling!
Perky Steady on!
Henry Come 'ere, Maria!

Henry pushes Mary onto the sofa

Mary (*relaxed, happy*) Don't you "Maria" me! I've had quite enough of that.

Henry (*embracing her*) I haven't had enough of anything, and neither have you.

Perky Excuse me, I'll go and get my case. Is there a maid's room with a lonely little single bed for me?

Henry Yes, you'll find it round at the back.

Perky Hope it's got a lonely little maid in it.

Perky exits through the front door

Henry I think we could actually steal a kiss at last.

Mary (*grabs him hungrily*) I want more than a kiss. I want all of you, *now!*

Mary pulls Henry down on top of her on the sofa and they begin to kiss passionately

Celia, minus her raffia bag, enters through the french windows

Celia I couldn't get round the side . . . (*She stops and utters a cry at what she sees*) Aahh!

Henry and Mary freeze immediately, her legs high in the air

Henry, what in Heaven's name do you think you're doing?

Henry Giving her the kiss of life!

Henry begins to give Mary mouth to mouth resuscitation

Celia What happened?

Henry She just keeled over and went down like a log.

Henry resumes blowing vigorously

Celia She's not a balloon, you know. Get out of the way, Henry. You obviously know nothing about first aid.

Henry Do you?

Celia Yes.

Celia pushes Henry out of the way and straddles Mary on the sofa

Henry Mount her gently, Mother dear.

Celia It looks to me like cardiac arrest.

Celia now gives Mary the correct massage—which looks to be extremely painful

Chitto enters through the french windows and is amazed at what he sees. He turns on his heel and exits again

Perky enters through the front door. He tiptoes down, unseen by Celia and Henry. He taps Henry on the shoulder causing Henry to jump and whirl round

Henry Aaaaagh!

Perky Aaaaagh!
Celia Be quiet, Henry! (*She looks at Mary*) I think she's responding. She's
going very red in the face. You'd better break the news to her husband.
Henry Who?

Perky is grinning broadly, obviously enjoying Henry's predicament

Celia Her *husband*! (*She indicates Perky with a jerk of her head*) He doesn't
seem to understand the gravity of the situation.
Henry Oh, yes. Pedro, you must steely yourself. (*He puts a comforting arm
round Perky's shoulders*) Maria keely over. Kaput.

*Perky sinks to his knees, beats his breast and howls with mid-European
fervour, combined with a touch of the Wailing Wall*

Celia (*still massaging*) You fool, Henry! Now he thinks she's dead.
Perky Aaah, Dead! Dead! (*He beats his head on the floor*) Finito! Kaput!
Henry How do you say "cardiac arrest" in Hungarian?
Perky (*agonised*) Hungarian! (*He beats his head again*) Aaah!
Celia (*pumping even harder*) I—don't—know.

Mary, having had enough, gives a yell

Mary Ahhhh!
Celia She's rallying.

Mary brushes Celia to one side and sits up, very much alive

Henry Good work, Mumpots!
Celia I think her husband should take over now.

*Henry looks at Perky and nods towards the kitchen door. Perky steers Mary
towards the kitchen*

   Mary exits

Perky Scusa Mumpotsky, Pedro molto gratinee, Mumpotty, per stoppy the
cardiacky arresti with budapesty on the balalikas. (*He picks up the tea
tray, goes to the kitchen door, and calls out*) Maria ina in cuccina poco
poco 'ave a cup of cocoa.

   Perky exits into the kitchen

Henry (*kissing Celia*) You've saved a precious life. Isn't it time you were on
your way?
Celia Oh yes, so it is.
Henry Too bad.

Henry hurries Celia towards front door

Celia (*stopping*) Would you like to know what I think about Maria?
Henry Not really, no.
Celia It was a fainting fit. She's probably pregnant.
Henry Oh, God! I hope not!
Celia (*laughing*) If she is it's her husband who should be worried, not you!

Celia moves towards front door

Henry No, he'll be absolutely delighted.
Celia I doubt it since he's been away for a year waiting for that bus in Budapest.

Celia blows him a kiss and exits through the front door

Henry closes the front door behind her

Leslie and Eve enter from the bedroom DL. *Eve his holding a bedspring. Leslie is rubbing his behind*

Eve Would you believe it? A Portuguese bedspring portugoosed him.

Perky pops his head out of the kitchen

Perky All clear?
Henry Yes. No more lies about who is who!

Perky and Mary enter from the kitchen

Leslie and Eve come DC

Perky Good-oh!
Henry So we can breathe again.
Mary You're lucky. I can't. She's cracked three of my ribs.
Henry Well, you can still swallow. Have a drink. It's thirsty work, lying.
Leslie I've got to hand it to you, Henry. What a performance!
Henry Thanks. Well, nothing else can go wrong.
Chitto (*off*) Ahoy there!
All (*together*) Wrong!

Chitto enters through the french windows with his clipboard and Celia's raffia bag

Chitto I smell champagne.

Chitto neatly tilts the bottle held in Henry's hands and fills his own glass

Has Mrs Peewit gone?
Henry Yes.
Chitto Oh. We were chatting by the pool and she left this bag behind, but she can pick it up when she comes back.
Leslie She's not coming back.
Henry (*happy as Larry*) She certainly is not.
Chitto She certainly is—with her surprise.
Henry What surprise?
Chitto Now, wait a minute. Am I supposed to tell you or not? It's one of the two. Oh, well, you're going to find out soon enough, anyway.
Mary What are you talking about?
Chitto Hang on a minute while I check. Yes. Has anyone here got a wife called Catherine?
Henry That depends. Why?
Chitto Well, her mother's gone to fetch her and bring her here.

Henry (*laughs*) All the way from England?
Chitto No, from the village, of course.
Henry The village?
Chitto Yes. She been having her hair done.
Henry Catherine's coming up here?
Chitto Yes. Try to adopt a look of joyful surprise.
Henry Surprise! Action stations, back to square one. (*Taking a glass from each of them in turn*) Pedro, Maria, Piers, Amanda. (*To Chitto*) You're you, and I'm me.
Mary Keep calm, Henry.

Henry, loaded with glasses, takes them to the bar

Perky Wait! I can't go on being the Hungarian houseboy. Catherine knows me. (*He indicates Eve*) And knows my real wife.
Eve So I can't be her.
Leslie And I can't be him.
Mary And Heaven knows who I can be?
Henry (*devastated*) Sunk! Completely sunk! Nobody can be anybody.

Chitto rises, puts on his hat

Chitto Well, you seem to be sorting things out nicely. I must be going. (*He squints at his watch*) Good Lord! Happy hour already.

Chitto takes the bottle of disinfectant from his pocket and is about to drink from the bottle when his eyes is caught by the label

What an extraordinary way to spell gin!

Chitto exits through the front door

Henry I don't know about the rest of you, but I'm going to hang myself.
Perky Hold it. You can still be okay if we four *all* slip out of the house and leave you to greet Catherine and Mumpots alone.
Henry How does that help?
Perky Celia thinks these two were the Marchbanks. You just tell her they've slipped out for a tête-a-tête dinner.
Henry That's a bit rude, isn't it?
Perky No, you dumb cluck! You're not supposed to *know* Mumpots is coming back.
Henry Of course. That's right!
Perky Pedro has taken Maria to the doctor's about her heart.
Henry Brilliant! Foolproof! Off you all go, then.
Eve No. Les and I are not setting foot outside this house.
Henry Why not?
Eve Because you won't let us back in.
Henry What if I gave you my word as a lawyer?
Leslie That settles it.
Henry Splendid!
Leslie We won't budge an inch.
Henry You miserable little . . .

Mary Henry, there's a car coming. They're here.
Henry Sunk!
Perky (*to Leslie and Eve*) Look, would you play along if we all hid somewhere *inside* the house?
Leslie Yes, I think we would.
Henry Hide? Where?
Perky Anywhere.
Eve Hopefully in one of the bedrooms.
Henry Don't be stupid! Catherine's bound to look all around.

Perky throws open the door of the cupboard

Perky What's in here?
Leslie Curtain cupboard.
Perky Marvellous. Come on.

Outside there is the sound of brakes and a babble of voices

Henry, in the absence of staff, you'll take Catherine and Mumpots out to a slap-up dinner. We can then escape at leisure.
Henry Right. I'll have them out of here in five minutes. (*Henry ushers the others into the cupboard*) In there, all of you.
Eve I don't fancy being stuffed in a cupboard.
Leslie Oh, come on! You've fancied it everywhere else.

Henry closes the cupboard door

Chitto enters through the front door

Chitto (*loudly*) Charlesworth!
Henry (*whirling round, startled*) Not Guilty!
Chitto I just bumped into your wife.
Henry (*faintly*) Have you?
Chitto Actually into her foot—ran over it.
Celia (*off*) Commander, lend a hand, will you?
Chitto Coming.

Chitto moves back to the front door

Celia appears, assisting Catherine (Kit), who is hobbling badly and is evidently in pain

Henry goes to her and kisses her

Henry My poor Kit!
Kit Oh, Henry darling! I was hoping to give you such a lovely surprise.
Henry Well you have!
Kit Oh, this ankle is agony. Can I sit down?
Henry No, you cannot. We must get you to a hospital at once.
Kit There's no need . . .
Henry Don't argue! Commander, how far is the furthest nearest hospital?
Chitto Eighty miles.
Kit Eighty miles!

Henry No time to waste. On our way.

Henry makes as if to wheel them out of front door again. Celia stops him

Celia Don't be silly, Henry. We'll call in the local doctor.
Kit And just let me rest up here.
Henry *Here*?!
Celia Why not? You have the place for a whole week.

Henry moves to the vicinity of the cupboard

Henry (*shouting*) A week!
Celia Don't shout. Let's get her onto the sofa.
Kit In fact, I think I'll *sleep* on the sofa.

Henry yells louder for the benefit of those in the cupboard

Henry Sleep, here, on the sofa!
Kit It's only for a week.
Henry For a *week*!
Kit You're so restless in bed.

Celia helps Kit onto the sofa

Celia Yes, the sofa's the best place.
Henry (*beginning to crack*) Don't interfere, Mumpots.
Celia If you share a bed you might kick her in the night.
Henry I could kick her in the ... (*Controlling himself*) Mumpots, how can I
cope with Kit on the sofa for a whole week?
Celia You won't have to cope. You have Pedro and Maria.
Henry No, I haven't. I just fired them.
Celia Why?
Henry It's a long story and I don't want to hear it.
Kit Could I have some extra cushions for my ankle?
Chitto I'll have a dekko in the cushion cupboard.
Celia And while you're about it, could you find a pouffe or something so
she can sit upright?
Chitto Pouffe? Right. I'll have a look in the pouffe cupboard.

Chitto moves, quickly for once—straight to the cupboard door

Henry (*agonised*) NO!

*Chitto, before Henry can stop him, opens the cupboard door. Leslie, Eve,
Perky and Mary now come out in single file. They are draped in four identical
curtains with black bands round their heads. Their faces are obscured. They
resemble Arabs. They start to walk across the room*

Celia (*rising*) Who on earth ... ?
Henry (*frantically*) MOROCCAN POUFFES!

*All the "Arabs" stick out a limp wrist as they move with gathering speed
towards the french windows and exit via the balcony*

CURTAIN

FURNITURE AND PROPERTY LIST

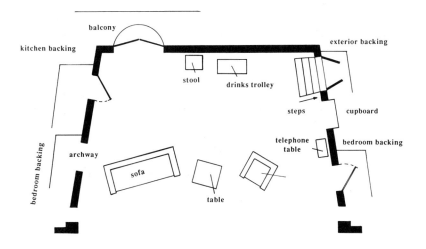

ACT I

On stage: Sofa

Armchair. *In it:* pair of smashed spectacles

Drinks trolley. *On it:* one banana, two halves of lemon, two tall tumblers, four whisky tumblers, jug of water and tumbler, soda syphon, bottles of gin, scotch, sherry, some fruit juices and tonic, unlabelled bottle of black liquid

Stool. *On it:* food hamper containing twelve bottles of green liquid (*Note: one bottle is drunk*)

Occasional tables—two. *On one:* telephone with press-button dial and long lead on handset, Portuguese directory, jackplug on lead. *On the other:* bowl of fruit including banana, lemon and one practical apple, handbell

Table lamps—one or two

French windows: open weave curtains—to fall off rail, moveable exterior shutters

Waste-paper basket

Two pictures

Button on wall—to "operate" electric curtains

Wall light

Bolt on kitchen door

Off stage L: Curtains and rod (**Chitto**)
Two suitcases (**Henry**)
Two suitcases (**Leslie**)

Off stage R: Curtains and rod (**Chitto**)
Plastic shopping with champagne and groceries (**Leslie**)
Eve's shoe without heel (**Leslie**)
Plastic shopping bag with groceries (**Eve**)
Change of clothes, carving knife, dustpan and brush (**Mary**)
Change of clothes, secateurs, chicken leg, wrapped sandwiches (**Henry**)

Personal: **Chitto:** clipboard with notepad, Panama hat, brief-case, spectacles, dictation recorder, watch
Leslie: white shirt
Mary: sheet of paper
Henry: binoculars
Celia: raffia beach bag. *In it:* gas bill, banana, fly-swat, chocolate liqueurs; neck-chains carrying spectacles, perfume bottle, pen, fob watch etc

ACT II

Set: On trolley, hidden from view: one pint beer mug of reddish drink topped with fruit and one large banana

Off stage L: Piece of four-poster bed (**Leslie**)
Suitcase, large bedspring (**Eve**)
Four identical curtains made into Arab-style headgear with four headbands (**Eve, Mary, Leslie, Perky**)

Off stage R: **Celia's** raffia bag (**Chitto**)
Salver. *On it:* five glasses, four containing champagne (**Henry**)
Dustpan containing dust and brush, tray. *On it:* teapot, milk-jug, cup, saucer, plate of thick sandwiches (**Mary**)

Personal: **Mary:** headscarf
Perky: sunglasses, blazer, Harrovian tie (*available from Gieves & Hawkes, 1 Savile Row, London, W1*)

LIGHTING PLOT

Fittings required: wall lights

ACT I

To open: Late afternoon sunlight

No cues

ACT II

To open: as close of Act I

No cues

EFFECTS PLOT

ACT I

Cue 1   **Chitto** turns on light switch   (Page 2)
            Silent flash and puff of smoke

Cue 2   **Chitto** straightens a picture   (Page 2)
            Another picture falls off wall

Cue 3   **Chitto** presses button on wall R of entrance   (Page 2)
            Curtains slide open and drop right off curtain rail

Cue 4   **Eve:** "I have sometimes wondered."   (Page 8)
            Crash from bedroom DL

Cue 5   **Eve:** "That's all we need. What next?"   (Page 10)
            Telephone rings

Cue 6   **Leslie:** "Never mind. I feel better."   (Page 12)
            Crash from bedroom DR

Cue 7   **Chitto:** "No. The old brainbox."   (Page 18)
            Telephone rings

Cue 8   **Eve** exits into bedroom DL   (Page 28)
            Telephone rings

Cue 9   **Mary** exits DR   (Page 32)
            Doorbell rings

ACT II

Cue 10   **Celia:** "For a moment I thought you said cough pox!"   (Page 39)
            Crash from bedroom DR

Cue 11   **Eve:** "So forget Mister Nice Guy and put the screws on like they   (Page 41)
                did."
            Sound of plate being smashed in kitchen R

Cue 12   **Henry:** "I will, I promise. (*Vastly relieved*) Whew!   (Page 42)
            Sound of car crashing L

Cue 13   **Chitto:** ". . . was killed in cold blood by Pedro and Maria."   (Page 44)
            Crash from bedroom DL

Cue 14   **Chitto:** "By God, they're at it again!"   (Page 44)
            Crash from bedroom

Cue 15   **Henry:** "I gave her a crash course."   (Page 47)
            Crash from kitchen R

Cue 16   **Henry:** "How you feel about it?"   (Page 47)
            Sound of plate shattering in kitchen R

MADE AND PRINTED IN GREAT BRITAIN BY
LATIMER TREND & COMPANY LTD PLYMOUTH
MADE IN ENGLAND